Principles of

Risk-Based
Decision Making

ABS Consulting

Government Institutes
4 Research Place, Rockville, Maryland 20850, USA
Phone: (301) 921-2300
Fax: (301) 921-0373
Email: giinfo@govinst.com
Internet: http://www.govinst.com

This book is based on a document, *Risk Based Decision-making Guidelines,* developed by the U.S. Coast Guard. The material was greatly expanded and updated in 2001 from the original document in 1997, and we determined that this public domain information is of interest to the regulated community; therefore, we are publishing this material in order to serve those interested. We have modified some of the original content in order to make this product more generically applicable and less Coast Guard specific.

Risk assessment and risk management are important topics in industry and government. Because of limited resources and increasing demands for services, most organizations simply cannot continue business as usual. Even if resources are not decreasing, the need for continuous improvement drives change within most organizations. These same conditions exist within the United States Coast Guard (Coast Guard) and within the marine industry as a whole.

ISBN 0-86587-908-7
Printed in the United States of America

Contents

Chapter 1- Introduction to Risk-Based Decision Making 1

1.0 Definition of Risk-Based Decision Making 1

2.0 Do You Need Risk-Based Decision Making? 2

3.0 The Risk-Based Decision Making Process 4

4.0 Dealing With Information Precision, Uncertainty, and Resource Needs 8

5.0 Barriers to Risk-Based Decision Making 11

Chapter 2- Loss Prevention Basics 13

1.0 Loss Prevention Basics 13

2.0 Events Producing Casualties 27

3.0 What Is Human Error? 28

4.0 Introduction to Root Causes 32

Chapter 3- Principles of Risk Assessment 47

1.0 Characterizing Risk 47

2.0 Introduction to Risk Assessment Methods 65

Chapter 4- Principles of Risk Management 73

1.0 Risk Goals 73

2.0 Factors Affecting Risk Acceptance 74

3.0 Issues of Acceptable Risk 76

4.0 Risk Management Categories 78

5.0 Accident Prevention Options 79

Chapter 5- Principles of Risk Communication 83

1.0 Definition of Risk Communication 83

2.0 Risk Communication in the Risk-Based Decision Making Process 84

3.0 Risk Communication Cycle 85

4.0 Successful Risk Communication 87

5.0 Developing Key Messages 91

6.0 Dealing with an Angry Public 93

7.0 Working with the Media 95

Contents

Chapter 6- Risk Assessment Tools **99**

1.0 Commonly Used Risk Assessment Tools 99

2.0 Summary of Pareto Analysis 100

3.0 Summary of Checklist Analysis 103

4.0 Summary of Relative Ranking/Risk Indexing 111

5.0 Summary of Preliminary Risk Analysis 114

6.0 Summary of Change Analysis 117

7.0 Summary of What-If Analysis 119

8.0 Summary of Failure Modes and Effects Analysis (FMEA) 121

9.0 Summary of Hazard and Operability (HAZOP) Analysis 124

10.0 Summary of Fault Tree Analysis 126

11.0 Summary of Event Tree Analysis 130

12.0 Summary of Event and Causal Factor Charting 133

13.0 Summary of Preliminary Hazard Analysis 136

14.0 Overview of Influence Diagraming 138

Chapter 7- Decision Analysis Tools **145**

1.0 Summary of Decision Analysis Tools 145

2.0 Choosing Decision Analysis Tools 146

3.0 Summary of Voting Methods 147

4.0 Summary of Weighted Scoring Methods 150

5.0 Summary of Decision Trees 153

6.0 Other Decision Analysis Tools 158

Chapter 8- Managing a Risk Assessment Project **159**

1.0 Scoping a Risk Assessment 160

2.0 Identifying Stakeholders and the Risk Assessment Team 163

3.0 Preparing a Risk Assessment 165

4.0 Facilitating the Risk Assessment Meetings 167

5.0 Documenting the Risk Assessment Meetings 169

6.0 Writing the Risk Assessment Report 170

7.0 Validating the Risk Assessment with Available Data 172

8.0 Evaluating the Recommendations 174

9.0 Reviewing a Risk Assessment 177

Appendix A- Table for Applying the Risk-Based Decision Making

   Process *181*

Appendix B- Hazard Identification Guidesheet *185*

Appendix C- Human Error: A Marine Safety Example *197*

Appendix D- Acronym List and Glossary of Terms *207*

Acknowledgements

We gratefully acknowledge the important contribution that the Coast Guard's *Risk-based Decision-making Guidelines* makes to the marine industry. The Marine Safety, Security, and Environmental Protection Directorate of the Coast Guard and the Coast Guard's Research and Development Center jointly produced the *Guidelines* and are leading efforts to institutionalize risk-based decision making within the Coast Guard. Many Coast Guard personnel contributed in some form to the development of the Guidelines, but the following individuals were key leaders in the development effort:

Marine Safety and Environmental Protection
CDR Timothy Close
Mr. Joseph Myers
LCDR Duane Boniface

Research and Development
Mr. Bert Macesker
LCDR Scott Kuhaneck
LT Michael Mulligan
Mr. Brian Dolph
Mr. Warren Heerlein

We hope that this product makes their fine work more readily available to the marine industry.

We also want to highlight the role that ABS Consulting's Risk Consulting Division has played in the development, roll-out, and ongoing implementation of risk-based decision making with the Coast Guard and now broadly in the marine industry. The Coast Guard partnered with ABS Consulting's Knoxville Office to (1) research and apply the most applicable risk assessment/management tools for maritime applications and (2) prepare an effective document, the Second Edition of the *Risk-based Decision-making Guidelines*, to communicate these concepts/tools to Coast Guard personnel.

Since completing the *Guidelines*, the risk management experts from the Knoxville Office have been helping the Coast Guard institutionalize the use of risk-based decision making in the field and at Headquarters through (1) specialized training workshops and incorporation of these concepts/tools into other Coast Guard training, (2) facilitation of numerous issue-specific workshops tackling various high profile issues/concerns in ports/waterways around the country, and (3) operating the Coast Guard's risk-based decision-making help desk service.

Individuals from the Knoxville Office of ABS Consulting that played a key role in the development of the *Guidelines* include the following:

Mr. David Walker
Mr. Walt Hanson
Mr. Chuck Mitchell

Mr. Steven Schoolcraft
Mr. Myron Casada
Ms. Jill Farmer

Mr. Vernon Guthrie
Mr. Andy Huff

If you have questions about the information contained in this product or would like to talk about risk-based decision-making applications for your organization, please contact:

Mr. David Walker
10301 Technology Drive
Knoxville, TN 37932-3392
Phone: (865) 671-5802
Fax: (865) 966-5287
Email: dwalker@absconsulting.com

Chapter 1
Introduction to Risk-Based Decision Making

1.0 Definition of Risk-Based Decision Making

The best place to begin this *Introduction to Risk-Based Decision Making* is with the definition of risk-based decision making:

> *A process that organizes information about the possibility for one or more unwanted outcomes into a broad, orderly structure that helps decision makers make more informed management choices*

A process ...

Risk-based decision making involves a series of basic steps. It can add value to almost any situation, especially when the possibility exists for serious or catastrophic outcomes. The steps can be used at different levels of detail and with varying degrees of formality, depending on the situation. The *key* to using the process is in completing each step in the most *simple, practical way* to provide the information the decision maker needs. Some situations are so complex that detailed risk assessments are needed, but most can be addressed with more simple risk assessments.

... that organizes information about the possibility for one or more unwanted outcomes ...

This information about the possibility for one or more unwanted outcomes separates risk-based decision making from more traditional decision making. The consideration of possible losses for any set of stakeholders is unique to risk-based decision making. These losses can include such things as harmful effects on safety and health, the environment, property loss, or mission success. The risks for an engineered system or activity are determined by the types of possible losses, the frequency at which they are expected to occur, and the effects they might have. Although not certain, these possible losses present real risks that must be considered in most decision-making processes.

... into a broad, orderly structure ...

Most decisions require information not only about risk, but about other things as well. This additional information can include such things as cost, schedule requirements, and public perception. In risk-based decision making, all of the identifiable factors that affect a decision must be considered. The factors may have different levels of importance in the final decision. Therefore, an orderly decision analysis structure that considers more than just risk is necessary to give decision makers the information needed to make smart choices.

... that helps decision makers ...

The only purpose of risk-based decision making is to provide enough information to help someone make a more informed decision. The process focuses on organizing information for logical understanding. It does not replace the decision maker. Neither should it force the decision maker into burdensome risk assessments to gather information that is either irrelevant to the decision or too late to affect it.

... make more informed management choices

The goal of risk-based decision making is to help people make better, more logical choices without complicating their work or taking away their authority. A *good* decision made quickly is much better than a *perfect* decision made too late. Also, a *good* decision does not always result in a *good* outcome. The best we can hope for is to equip intelligent decision makers with good information based on a number of decision factors and the interests of stakeholders. On average, and over time, *good* decisions made through this process should provide the best outcomes. They will also provide logical explanations for decisions when the outcomes are not favorable.

2.0 Do You Need Risk-Based Decision Making?

We make hundreds of risk-based decisions every day:

- Should I change lanes on the interstate?
- How often should I change the oil in my car?
- What can I do to lower my risk of cancer?
- Can I put off this task until later without affecting my project?

For almost *every* decision, there is a chance for some unwanted outcome. We include this possibility in our decisions, along with the consequences of the unwanted outcomes and the effort that would be needed to make the unwanted outcomes less likely or less severe.

2.1 Informal risk-based decision making

For most of our decisions, we do not formally assess the likelihood and consequences of possible unfortunate outcomes. For example, we do not study traffic statistics before changing lanes. Instead, we rely on our *feel* for the situation to create a level of comfort. If we are uncomfortable, we look for ways to change the situation to make ourselves more comfortable with the risks. For these types of decisions, the risk-based decision-making process takes place within seconds and becomes second nature.

2.2 Formal risk-based decision making

For some decisions, we are more formal about assessing the frequencies and consequences of possible unwanted outcomes. For example, when we decide how to provide for our families in case we are injured or killed, we rate a number of factors, including the following:

- The possible losses we face (from short-term disabilities to death)

- The chances of those losses

- The economic consequences of those losses

- The ways in which we can protect against the effects of the losses; for example, we can buy insurance

- The acceptability of the risks and impacts of the protections; for example, can we afford the insurance or are we willing to give up certain extras?

For these types of decisions, the risk-based decision-making process is more structured and more defensible, but it takes more time.

2.3 To use or not to use

The question is not, "Should I use risk-based decision making in my industry?" The question is, "How can I use risk-based decision making most effectively for my needs?" These *Principles* present several tools used in risk-based decision making so that you can choose the most useful approach for you. Your emphasis should always be on using the most suitable tools for the situation, not just on following one approach. It is, however, important to follow some standard procedures and techniques for (1) improving the efficiency of your efforts, (2) ensuring that your approach is technically sound, and (3) gaining acceptance of your work from others.

Risk-based Decision Making

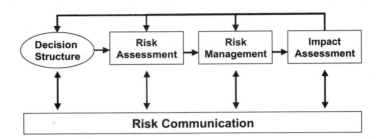

3.0 The Risk-Based Decision-making Process

Regardless of how formally you address risk-based decision making or the specific tools you use, risk-based decision making is made up of five major components, which are shown in the figure above.

Components of risk-based decision making

The following sections introduce the five components of risk-based decision making.

Step 1 — Establish the decision structure

Understanding and defining the decision that must be made is critical. This first component of risk-based decision making is often overlooked and deserves more discussion. The following steps must be performed to accomplish this critical component:

Step 1a — Define the decision. Specifically describe what decision(s) must be made. Major categories of decisions include (1) accepting or rejecting a proposed facility or operation, (2) determining who and what to inspect, and (3) determining how to best improve a facility or operation.

Step 1b — Determine who needs to be involved in the decision. Identify and solicit involvement from key stakeholders who (1) should be involved in making the decision or (2) will be affected by actions resulting from the decision-making process.

Step 1c — Identify the options available to the decision maker. Describe the choices available to the decision maker. This will help focus efforts only on issues likely to influence the choice among credible alternatives.

Step 1d — Identify the factors that will influence the decisions (including risk factors). Few decisions are based on only one factor. Most require consideration of many factors, including costs, schedules, risks, etc., at the same time. The stakeholders must identify the relevant decision factors.

Step 1e — Gather information about the factors that influence stakeholders. Perform specific analyses (e.g., risk assessments and cost studies) to measure against the decision factors.

Chapter 5 of this *Principles of Risk-Based Decision Making* provides an overview of common decision analysis tools to help you structure your overall decision-making process.

Step 2 — Perform the risk assessment

Different types of risk are important factors in many types of decisions. Very simply, risk assessment is the process of understanding the following:

- What bad things can happen

- How likely they are to happen

- How severe the effects may be

The bad things of interest can be safety and health losses, property losses, environmental losses, schedule impacts, political issues, etc.

Risk assessment can range from very simple, personal judgments by individuals to very complex assessments by expert teams using a broad set of tools and information, including historical loss data. The key to risk assessment is choosing the right approach to provide the needed information without overworking the problem. The following steps must be performed to assess risk:

Step 2a — Establish the risk-related questions that need answers. Decide what questions, if answered, would provide the risk insights needed by the decision maker.

Step 2b — Determine the risk-related information needed to answer the questions. Describe the information necessary to answer each question posed in the previous step. For each information item, specify the following:

- Information type needed

- Precision required

- Certainty required

- Analysis resources (staff-hours, costs, etc.) available

Step 2c — Select the risk analysis tool(s). Select the risk analysis tool(s) that will most efficiently develop the required risk-related information.

Step 2d — Establish the scope for the analysis tool(s). Set any appropriate physical or analytical boundaries for the analysis.

Step 2e — Generate risk-based information using the analysis tool(s). Apply the selected risk analysis tool(s). This may require the use of more than one analysis tool and may involve some iterative analysis (i.e., starting with a general, low-detail analysis and progressing toward a more specific, high-detail analysis).

Chapter 2 of this *Principles of Risk-based Decision Making* explores the topic of risk assessment in more detail.

Chapter 6 provides an overview of many of the most common risk assessment tools.

Step 3 — Apply the results to risk management decision making

One goal in most decision-making processes is to lower risk as much as possible. Sometimes the risk will be acceptable; at other times, the risk must change to become acceptable. To reduce risk, action must be taken to manage it. These actions must provide more benefit than they cost. They must also be acceptable to stakeholders and not cause other significant risks. The following steps must be performed to manage risk:

Step 3a — Assess the possible risk management options. Determine how the risks can be managed most effectively. This decision can include (1) accepting/rejecting the risk or (2) finding specific ways to reduce the risk.

Step 3b — Use risk-based information in decision making. Use the risk-related information within the overall decision framework to make an informed, rational decision. This final decision-making step often involves significant communication with a broad set of stakeholders.

Chapter 3 of this *Principles of Risk-based Decision Making* explores the topic of risk management in more detail.

Step 4 — Monitor effectiveness through impact assessment

Impact assessment is the process of tracking the effectiveness of actions taken to manage risk. The goal is to verify that the organization is getting the expected results from its risk management decisions. If not, a new decision-making process must be considered.

Step 5 — Facilitate risk communication

Risk communication is a two-way process that must take place during risk-based decision making. At every step in the process, encourage stakeholders to do the following:

Provide guidance on key issues to consider. Stakeholders identify the issues of importance to them. They present their views on how each step of the process should be performed, or at least provide comments on plans suggested by others.

Provide relevant information needed for assessments. Some or all of the stakeholders may have key information needed in the decision-making process.

Provide buy-in for the final decisions. Stakeholders should agree on the work to be done in each phase of the risk-based decision-making process. They can then support the ultimate decisions.

Chapter 4 of this *Principles of Risk-Based Decision Making* explores the topic of risk communication in more detail.

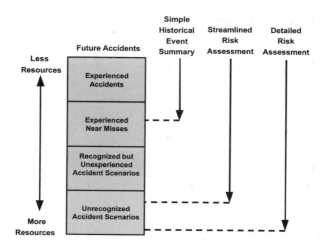

4.0 Dealing with Information Precision, Uncertainty, and Resource Needs

Information needed for decision making is characterized by its precision and certainty. The level of precision and certainty is balanced by our willingness to expend resources to obtain it. Generally, highly precise, highly certain information is very expensive to obtain.

To make risk-based decisions, the decision maker must understand how future accidents can occur. For example, information on historical performance may be available, but the decision maker believes that this information does not adequately predict the existence of other potential accidents. Therefore, the decision maker commissions a risk assessment to provide more certain information about future accidents. As expected, additional resources were expended to obtain this more certain information. As more certain, more precise information is required to predict future performance, more resources are required to obtain it.

4.1 Dealing with information precision

The precision of information is characterized by its level of detail. For example, a person can be from the United States, Texas, or Dallas. Likewise, a number can be described by the number of places following the decimal point. The more precise the information, the more detail is inherent in it.

The decision maker must understand the precision required to make a decision. If knowing that a person is from Texas is sufficient to make a decision, there is no need to expend resources to determine which city in Texas the person is from. Likewise, if numerical information to one decimal place is precise enough to make a decision, information precise to three decimal places will not affect it.

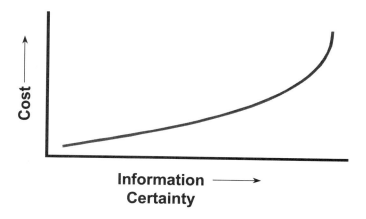

4.2 Dealing with information uncertainty

In any decision-making process, there is constant struggle between the need for more and better information and the practicality of improving the information. This is illustrated by the simple figure below.

Even when a lot of information is collected, a great deal of uncertainty remains. So the decision makers and information suppliers must work together to make sure that the cost of collecting more accurate data does not outweigh the benefits of having it. This is why analysts should *never* use very complex risk assessment tools without first trying to meet decision-making needs with simpler tools.

Dealing with uncertainty is part of any decision-making process. Therefore, those taking part in decision making, either directly or indirectly, must be aware of the most likely sources of uncertainty: model uncertainty and data uncertainty.

Model uncertainty

The models used in both the general decision-making structure and in detailed risk assessments will never be perfect. The detail in a model and scope boundaries will determine how well the model reflects reality. Even if the data are perfect, the model usually brings some doubt into the results.

For example, Phil was asked to describe what factors would influence his choice of a new car. If Phil cannot describe all of the factors that influence his choice, then these factors will not appear in his decision model.

More detailed levels of risk analysis can reduce model uncertainty by more thoroughly accounting for potentially important accident scenarios. However, more thorough analysis also costs more.

The simplest risk assessments are historical event summaries and account only for known accidents, and possibly some near misses, that have occurred during some reporting period. Streamlined risk assessments require more resources, but they also account for more near misses, as well as other recognized accident scenarios that did not occur. More detailed risk assessments require even more resources, but they systematically identify and account for previously unrecognized accident scenarios.

Data uncertainty

Data uncertainty causes much concern during decision making. Data uncertainty arises from any or all of the following:

- The needed data do not exist

- The analysts do not know where to collect the data, or they do not have the staff, funds, or time to collect it

- The quality of the data is questionable, usually because of the methods used to gather it

- The data vary widely, making their use complex

Although steps can be taken to reduce uncertainty in data, all data have some uncertainty. This uncertainty cannot be ignored. Following are methods available for dealing with data uncertainty:

Subjectively characterize uncertainty (for example, as high or low). A simple approach in which doubt in the final answer is estimated based on personal experience or belief.

Perform calculations using best-case and worst-case situations. An approach that uses different calculations for best-case and worst-case conditions to reflect the range of possible outcomes.

Analyze a number of possible situations (i.e., what-if scenarios). An expanded version of the previous approach that involves calculations for many other sets of conditions, usually including an estimate of how likely each set is to occur.

Decrease the precision requirements. Using broader ranges when categorizing the frequency and consequence of accidents increases the certainty in the selection.

Perform calculations using probability distributions in place of discrete estimates. A more complicated approach that uses statistics to describe data used in a model so that statistical descriptions of the expected outcomes can be formed.

Choose a simple method first for dealing with uncertainty. If decision makers need better estimates, the uncertainty can be reduced for the issues that most affect the model.

4.3 Dealing with resource needs

The objective is to use the minimum resources necessary to develop the required information. One effective means of minimizing resources involves starting with the lowest-cost approach that can possibly provide needed information with the required precision and certainty. This strategy most often relies on "streamlined" forms of traditional risk assessment tools. For example, before requesting any detailed modeling, the decision maker might contact one or more system experts and simply ask their perception of the answer to the risk-based question. Based on their experience, the experts may be able to provide the needed results with adequate precision and certainty. The need for more detailed analysis is therefore avoided. Be ready to commission more detailed risk assessments, though, if results from the less detailed approaches are not suitable for making a decision.

5.0 Barriers to Risk-Based Decision Making

A common barrier to risk-based decision making is the perception that mounds of highly precise, technical data are required before a decision can be made. Overcome this perceived barrier by trying to develop the data from information that is already at hand. Even though the precision and certainty of this data may not be high, they may be high enough for the decision maker. When more detailed data are required, then you know that you have at least tried to develop the required decision-making information from what was immediately available to you using the minimum resources.

Another common barrier to risk-based decision making is the perception that the risk assessment part of the process takes far too much time. There is no question that more time is required for complicated decisions that use information developed from highly precise and certain data. However, risk-based decisions are often not this complicated. Do existing risk-based decision-making tools like checklists and risk indexes work? These tools take very little time, but they often end up providing the information needed to make the decision.

One impediment to risk-based decision making is found in the culture of "it's always been done this way." Challenge this thinking. Why has it always been done this way? Do regulations REQUIRE this decision to be made this way, or is this simply a convenient interpretation of a flexible rule?

Sometimes the prescriptive requirements that appear to be inflexible can be changed. Use the risk-based decision-making process to help change prescriptive requirements that do not effectively manage important risks.

Risk-based decision making is for *everyone*. An inexperienced person given basic training in the use of a well-developed risk-based checklist will make good risk-based decisions. Tear down barriers that cause people to believe risk-based decision making is only for the most experienced. Use the experienced people to help develop information for complex decisions and to create new risk-based decision-making tools. No one should perceive experience as a barrier to risk-based decision making.

Chapter 2
Loss Prevention Basics

1.0 Loss Prevention Basics

Before you can learn to perform risk assessments, you need to understand how casualties occur and how they can be prevented.

What is a casualty?

A casualty is any event associated with a system that leads to adverse effects on workers, the public, property, commerce, or the environment. Casualties have the following characteristics:

- They are unplanned

- They involve human errors, equipment failures, or external events

- They have an impact on the economy, safety and health, or the environment

- They generally have underlying root causes that create error-likely situations for people and conditions leading to equipment failure

- They are frequently preceded by related events that can be detected and corrected

- They will always be possible, but can be effectively managed

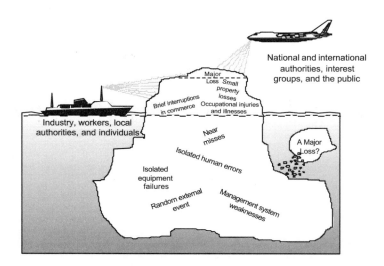

1.1 Loss prevention iceberg

The loss prevention iceberg is an effective model for understanding casualties. The following sections describe how different groups view the events that make up the iceberg.

Iceberg structure

Top. The top of the iceberg is a small but critical area representing major losses. Major casualties are usually caused by many of the same problems that cause less severe, but more frequent, day-to-day problems.

Visible remainder. The visible remainder above the water is a significant area representing the day-to-day casualties that produce safety, environmental, or economic losses.

Shallow submerged. The shallow submerged area represents abnormal events that almost resulted in losses. Generally, these near misses largely outnumber actual day-to-day casualties and can be considered prior events leading to actual losses.

Deeper submerged. The deeper submerged area represents the many human errors, equipment failures, and external events that cause casualties and near misses.

Bottom. The bottom of the iceberg represents the underlying management system weaknesses that create the following:

- Error-likely situations for people

- Conditions leading to equipment failures

- Inadequate protections against external events

Different views of loss prevention

People see parts of the loss prevention iceberg differently.

- **National and international authorities, interest groups, and the public.** These people focus on the top of the iceberg to avoid major casualties, or large numbers of less severe casualties, that threaten the organization or lead to significant negative publicity. They leave less severe casualties and loss prevention management to others.

- **Industry, workers, local authorities, and individuals.** These people focus on the visible remainder of the iceberg to reduce routine casualties that impact productivity and cause management headaches. They pay attention to events that almost cause casualties (i.e., near misses), although they usually have trouble seeing these events. They have difficulty finding the time and resources to investigate and prevent the underlying problems.

Buoyancy principle as a guide for loss prevention

- Removing large portions of the iceberg above the water causes the iceberg to rise. Addressing only the visible events helps reduce the size of the iceberg, but it will rise and make other events (actual casualties) visible.

- Removing portions of the iceberg below the water causes the iceberg to sink. Addressing the underlying problems helps reduce the size of the iceberg and the number of visible events (actual casualties) above the water.

Remember, we cannot get rid of the entire iceberg. Even if there are no visible problems, danger still exists below the water. Major events can also break off from the iceberg without warning. However, our attention must certainly focus on identifying and correcting the underlying root causes of our loss exposures as represented by the portion of the iceberg below the waterline. We clearly cannot simply wait until types of casualties become visible, by actually causing loss, and then taking actions to prevent recurrence.

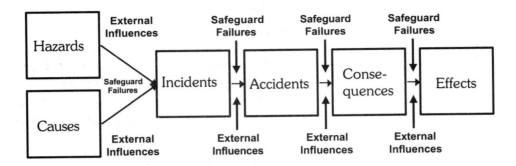

1.2 The accident sequence: Elements of a casualty

Casualties usually occur through a chain of events ending in one or more unwanted effects. This chain of events begins with *hazards* capable of causing casualties. If there are no hazards, there are no casualties. An equipment failure, human error, or external event is necessary for a hazard to cause an accident (i.e., a casualty). Some refer to this *initiating event* as an *incident*. Sometimes one or more equipment failures, human errors, or external events must take place after the initial incident (i.e., the initiating event) for an accident to occur. An accident has at least one unwanted *consequence* with a measurable *effect*. This outcome is influenced throughout the chain of events by the presence of *safeguards* and their success or failure.

Causes are the underlying reasons why the initial incident occurs and safeguard failures allow the chain of events to progress. These are sometimes also called root causes of the accident. The following pages describe the chain of events in more detail.

Definitions of terms commonly used in risk assessment

Hazards — Situations, conditions, characteristics, or properties that create the possibility of unwanted consequences

Incidents or initiating events — Events in an accident sequence that begin a chain of events. This chain of events will result in one or more unwanted consequences with measurable effects unless planned safeguards interrupt the progression of the chain.

Accidents — Casualties

Consequences — Unwanted events that can negatively affect subjects of interest. These include property damage or loss, worker injury or illness, loss of commerce, etc.

Effects — Measurable negative impacts on subjects of interest (i.e., the magnitudes of the consequences)

Safeguards — Planned protections that are intended to interrupt the progression of accident sequences at various points in accident chains of events. Safeguards can be applied as barriers at any or all of the transitions (i.e., arrows) in the accident sequence model. These planned protections may be physical devices, human interventions, or administrative policies.

Causes — Underlying reasons why the initial incident occurs and safeguards fail to interrupt the chain of events. The causes, sometimes called root causes, are typically weaknesses in management systems, which create error-likely situations for people and vulnerabilities in equipment.

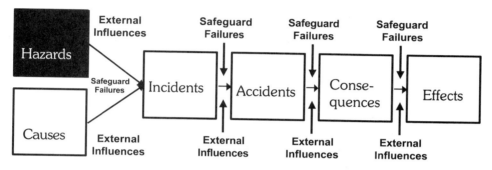

1.2.1 Elements of a casualty: Hazards

The following sections describe the major categories of hazards.

Combustible or flammable hazards. Combustible or flammable hazards exist when there is the potential for one or more materials to quickly react with air or some other oxidant, releasing energy in the form of heat and light.

Examples:

- Hydrocarbons and hydrocarbon derivatives (oil, LNG, LPG, etc.)
- Hydrogen
- Other gases (e.g., carbon monoxide)
- Finely powdered nonflammable materials
- Various metals (depending on the oxidizer)
- Wood products
- Cloth materials

Explosion hazards. Explosion hazards exist when there is the potential for one or more substances to release energy over a short period of time, creating a pressure wave that travels away from the source.

Examples:

- Many flammable materials
- Powders and dusts
- Nitrates
- Peroxides
- Compressed or liquefied gases
- Highly reactive materials
- Strong oxidizers
- Cryogenic liquids

Toxic hazards. Toxic hazards exist when there is the potential for one or more materials to cause biological damage to surrounding organisms by being absorbed through the skin, inhaled, eaten, or injected.

Examples:

- Chlorine or bromine
- Cleaning and maintenance fluids
- Contaminated food, water, and medical supplies

Asphyxiant hazards. Asphyxiant hazards exist when there is the potential for one or more materials to prevent organisms from breathing.

- **Simple asphyxiants.** Simple asphyxiants are usually nontoxic gases that replace the oxygen necessary to support life. Common simple asphyxiants are carbon dioxide and nitrogen.

- **Chemical asphyxiants.** Chemical asphyxiants are materials that stop organisms from using oxygen. Carbon monoxide is a chemical asphyxiant that prevents hemoglobin from carrying oxygen.

Corrosivity hazards. A corrosivity hazard exists when there is the potential for one or more materials to chemically burn body tissues, especially the skin and eyes, or to excessively erode or dissolve materials of construction or emergency response equipment.

Examples:

- Cleaning and maintenance fluids
- Battery acid
- Bleach

Chemical reactant hazards. A chemical reactant hazard exists when there is the potential for one or more materials to chemically combine, or to self-react, and produce unwanted consequences.

Examples:

- The side-by-side storage of reactive materials
- Reactive contaminants in materials

Principles of Risk-Based Decision Making

Thermal hazards. A thermal hazard exists when there is the potential for very hot or cold temperatures to produce unwanted consequences affecting people, materials, equipment, or work areas.

Examples:

- Exposed or uninsulated high- or low-temperature equipment or materials
- Fires or explosions
- Chemical reactions
- Extreme ambient conditions and other equipment or operations in the area
- Phase changes
- Gas compression or expansion
- Friction

Potential energy hazards. Potential energy hazards exist when unwanted consequences can result from the following:

- High pressures other than explosions (e.g., normal operational pressures)
- Low pressures (e.g., vacuum conditions)
- Mass, gravity, or height (e.g., lifting operations)

Kinetic energy hazards. Kinetic energy hazards exist when unwanted consequences can result from motion of materials, equipment, or vehicles.

Electrical energy hazards. Electrical energy hazards exist when unwanted consequences can result from contact with, or failure of, manufactured or natural sources of electrical voltage or current. Examples include lightning, electrical charges, short circuits, stray currents, and loss of power sources.

19

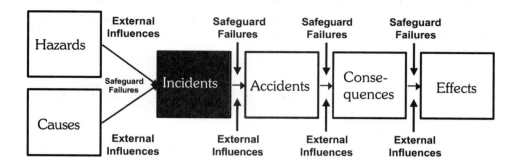

1.2.2 Elements of a casualty: Incidents (initiating events)

Incidents are also known as initiating events. They start the actual chain of events leading to casualties. In some cases, this chain of events can be quite long, when many layers of protection exist against losses.

Incidents can be equipment failures, human errors, external influences, or any action or occurrence.

Often, an initial incident challenges protective features that also must fail before an incident can become an accident. These special types of safeguards are call **demanded events.** Demanded events can be failed responses to initiating events by equipment or humans. Sometimes, other external events or conditions also influence the progress of an event chain and can be considered a demanded event.

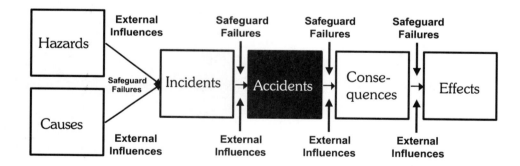

1.2.3 Elements of a casualty: Accidents (casualties)

The undesired casualties that are possible when a chain of events is completed can be classified in many ways.

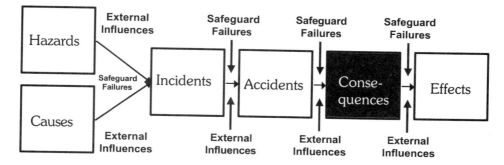

1.2.4 Elements of a casualty: Consequences

Casualties can result in different types of losses for various stakeholders. Some of these consequences include worker safety and health impacts (e.g., injuries or illnesses), public safety and health impacts (e.g., injuries or illnesses), Economic impacts (property damage or loss of commerce), and environmental impacts (releases of contaminants, such as oil or other hazardous materials)

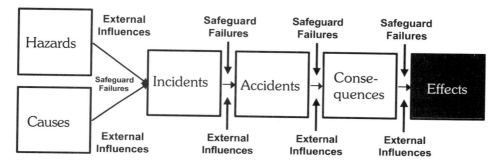

1.2.5 Elements of a casualty: Effects

The levels of effect related to consequences can be classified in many ways. The following table provides an example of how the Coast Guard has characterized levels of effect in at least one risk analysis.

Example Types of Effects*				
Severity	Safety Impact	Environmental Impact	Economic Impact	Mission Impact
Major (1)	One or more deaths or permanent disability	Releases that result in long-term disruption of the ecosystem or long-term exposure to chronic health risks	≥ $3M	≥ $3M
Moderate (2)	Injury that requires hospitalization or lost work days	Releases that result in short-term disruption of the ecosystem	≥$10K and <$3M	≥$10K and <$3M
Minor (3)	Injury that requires first aid	Pollution with minimal acute environmental or public health impact	≥ $100 and <$10K	≥ $100 and <$10K

* Losses in these categories result from both immediate and long-term effects (e.g., considering both acute and chronic effects when evaluating safety and health).

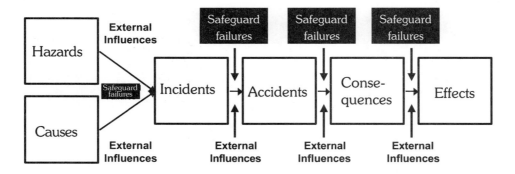

1.2.6 Elements of a casualty: Safeguards

Safeguards can be engineered systems, human monitoring and response, or administrative policies and programs for (1) reducing hazards, (2) preventing incidents, (3) interrupting chains of events before casualties occur, (4) reducing consequences, or (5) reducing effects. Safeguards, especially administrative safeguards, also help eliminate the underlying causes of the events in the accident chain.

Examples:

- Preventive maintenance for equipment
- Policy requiring a safety supervisor for all operations
- Personnel qualification programs for key positions
- Inspections

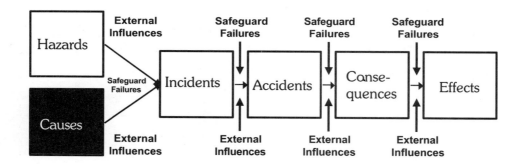

1.2.7 Elements of a casualty: Causes

The chain of events leading to an accident typically involves a series of human errors, equipment failures, and external influences. However, these are seldom the true causes of the accidents. Organizational issues, often referred to as management system weaknesses, are really the root causes of most accidents. Examples of these root causes include, but are certainly not limited to, the following:

For equipment failures:

- Inappropriate design or application
- Lack of predictive or preventive maintenance
- Erroneous repairs
- Unrecognized or ill-advised equipment changes

For human errors:

- Wrong, confusing, or missing procedures
- Lack of, wrong, or incomplete training
- Poor human/system interfaces
- Poor work conditions
- Excessive workload
- Lack of or deficient communication systems or processes
- Lack of or deficient supervision
- Poor workplace culture and motivational issues

For external influences

- Failing to anticipate and protect against reasonably foreseeable external conditions such as poor weather

Case study: The Exxon Valdez accident

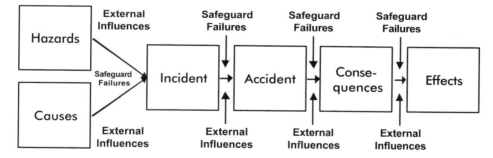

1.3 Case study: The Exxon Valdez accident

In 1989, a major oil spill occurred in Prince William Sound, Alaska, when the Exxon Valdez ran aground while leaving the Aleyeska Marine Terminal. The following sections describe the chain of events involved in this catastrophic loss.

Hazards

- Oil (environmental pollutant and toxin)

- Kinetic energy of vessel

Incident (initiating event)

- The captain ordered the helmsman to leave the shipping lanes to steer around icebergs

Accident

- Vessel ran aground

Consequences

- 600-foot hole ripped in the bottom of the tanker
- 240,000 barrels (10,000,000 gallons) of oil spilled, causing catastrophic damage to the local environment

Effects

- Major environmental damage, including many dead animals
  - 1,000+ otters
  - 35,000+ birds
- $1 billion+ in cleanup costs

Long-range impacts

- Environmental damage to Prince William Sound
- Fishing fleet in area affected
- Increased public concern about transportation accidents, especially in ship traffic in Prince William Sound

Failed safeguards and external influences

- The captain left orders with the third mate to turn back into the shipping lanes at a certain point, and the captain then left the bridge
- The third mate failed to order the new helmsman to turn back into the shipping lanes at the point prescribed by the captain
- Captain not on bridge
- Experienced mate not in charge of critical turn
- First cleanup team did not arrive until 14 hours after the spill
  - *dedicated* recovery barge had been in dry dock for repairs for the last 2 months
  - booms and skimmer equipment had to be located and loaded onto barge
  - once loaded, the barge was unloaded to transport pumps needed to transfer oil from the Exxon Valdez to another ship
- Dispersants to be used on spill
  - worldwide supply was not large enough for this size of spill
  - authorization to use dispersants was not given for 3 days
- Response was disorganized because of lack of planning; 48 hours after the spill, only 3,000 of 240,000 barrels of oil were recovered

Safeguards not provided

- Double hull tanker
  - double hull may not have prevented the spill, but could have reduced the consequences and effects
- Effective Coast Guard monitoring capability

Case Study: The NASA Challenger accident

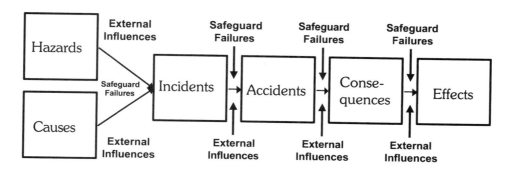

1.4 Case study: The NASA Challenger accident

In 1986, the space shuttle Challenger exploded 73 seconds after lift-off from the Kennedy Space Center in Florida. The following sections describe the chain of events involved in this catastrophic loss.

Hazard

- Fire and explosion hazards of fuels (liquid hydrogen and liquid oxygen)

Incident (initiating event)

- Lift-off of a shuttle when the ambient temperature was low

Accident

- Flight 51-L explodes 73 seconds after lift-off

Consequences

- Loss of seven astronauts
- Loss of a multi-billion-dollar shuttle

Effects

- Seven fatalities
- Multi-billion dollar economic loss
- Major impact on shuttle program

Long-range impacts
- Suspension of the shuttle program for almost three years
- Safety culture of NASA considered suspect

Failed safeguards and external influences
- Solid rocket motor rubber O-ring failed to seal properly because of its reduced pliability from sitting at a low temperature prior to launch
- Heavy wind shear during the last 45 seconds of the flight caused higher than normal bending of the joints of the solid rocket motor sealed by the rubber O-ring
- High-pressure hot exhaust gases from the solid rocket motor eroded through the cold rubber O-ring (aided by the higher-than-normal bending of the joint) and contacted the external fuel tank
- Ineffective management assessment of identified issues
  - temperature effects on O-rings not well understood by launch safety personnel
  - no definite operating envelope was set for O-rings
  - design specification did not include a temperature range
- Prior evidence of O-ring problems was not viewed as a problem
  - O-ring damage was observed on 15 of 25 missions
  - eventually, O-ring damage was viewed as acceptable

Safeguards not provided
- Effective O-ring design
- Timely communication of temperature limit for O-rings in this service

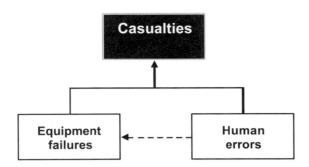

2.0 Events Producing Casualties

A casualty is caused by a combination of one or more equipment failures or human errors.

The keys to preventing accidents are (1) understanding the combinations of events leading to an accident and (2) knowing how to make the equipment failures and human errors less likely.

There is an entire science dedicated to forensic analysis of equipment failures, which is more than could be addressed in these *Principles*. However, a good technical knowledge of equipment failure mechanisms is often important for identifying and managing risks.

Often overlooked is the importance of human error prevention in risk management. In fact, human error is also the underlying cause of most equipment failures. After all, who designs, builds, manufactures, installs, operates, and maintains the equipment? People! Because of the importance of human error in risk management, section 3 of this chapter explores human error in more detail. Of course, there is also a whole field of study dedicated to preventing human errors and improving human performance.

Human Error Categories

Intentional

O m i s s i o n	Don't lubricate the bearing	Add a little extra grease	C o m m i s s i o n
	Forget to lubricate the bearing	Add the wrong grease	

Unintentional

3.0 What is Human Error?

The term "human error" refers to human actions or inactions outside the tolerances established by a system, even if no immediate consequences occur. Systems within every industry are almost always subject to failure as a result of human error.

Human error includes the following:

• Personnel not following procedures or neglecting routine duties

• Improper or inadequate training of workers

• Errors in writing operating instructions

• Equipment or system design, construction, or installation errors

• Improper or inadequate inspection, testing, or repair of equipment

• Lack of management oversight

Human error excludes *deliberate actions performed with harmful intentions (i.e., sabotage).*

A human error is typically characterized by the following descriptions:

Error of omission. Failure to perform a task or step

Error of commission. Performing a task or step incorrectly, as in the following:

• Selection error
  – selects wrong display or device
  – mispositions device
  – issues wrong command or information
  – too slow

Extraneous act

Sequence error
  – too soon
  – too late

Time error
  – too long
  – too short

Quantitative error
  – too little
  – too much
  – too fast

Unintentional error. An action committed or omitted *accidentally*, with no prior thought

Intentional errors. An intentional error does *not* include sabotage. The difference is in the *motive*. This error includes the following:

- An action committed or omitted deliberately, because of a perception that there is a better or equally effective way to perform the task or step. This is often a *shortcut* that may not be recognized as a mistake until other conditions arise that result in a noticeable problem.

  An action committed or omitted because the worker *misdiagnosed* the system's problem or need. At best, such an action delays the correct response; at worst, it compounds the problem.

Unintentional error. An action committed or omitted *accidentally*, with no prior thought

Intentional error. An intentional error does *not* include sabotage. The difference is in the *motive*. This error includes the following:

An action committed or omitted deliberately, because of a perception that there is a better or equally effective way to perform the task or step. This is often a *shortcut* that may not be recognized as a mistake until other conditions arise that result in a noticeable program.

An action committed or omitted because the worker *misdiagnosed* the system's problem or need. At best, such an action delays the correct response; at worst, it compounds the problem.

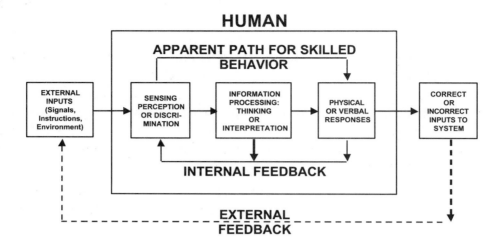

3.1 Simple model of human behavior

Human interaction with a system can be modeled as a component with three distinct functions. The rest of the system continuously provides information that enters the human through one of our five senses.

1. **Sensor, perception, or discrimination.** The brain filters out most external inputs as irrelevant information. The first task of the human "component" is to recognize important information and discriminate it from background noise.

2. **Information processing: thinking or interpretation.** The human must then process the input to determine its meaning and to select an appropriate response. When people practice the same response to a given input, they eventually appear to bypass this function (i.e., the apparent path for skilled behavior). This is when actions become second nature and explains why simply retraining and improving procedures often does not improve human performance.

3. **Physical or verbal responses.** Finally, the human physically responds based on the perceived or processed information. Lack of action is also a response.

The response in turn provides new inputs to the human who can sense his or her own actions (internal feedback) and sense how the system is responding (external feedback). Well-designed systems react perceptibly to the new input and provide feedback to the human by altering the external inputs.

```
┌─────────────────────────────────────────────────────────┐
│                                                           │
│            Results of error-likely situations            │
│                                                           │
│          ■ Lack of external input                        │
│          ■ Failure to sense input                        │
│          ■ Misinterpretation of input                    │
│          ■ Inappropriate response                        │
│          ■ Lack of feedback                              │
│                                                           │
└─────────────────────────────────────────────────────────┘
```

3.2 Results of error-likely situations

Error-likely situations can exist at any element of the human performance model.

Lack of external input such as signals or instructions. The person doesn't know that he or she should act because there is no signal provided to the user.

Failure to sense input. An input signal is provided but is not sensed because of information overload, insufficient discrimination, or poorly organized information. Information presented to the user must be organized and prioritized. Important and urgent inputs must stand out from others. Training and experience can increase the likelihood that appropriate signals are identified, but system design is the key to correcting these issues.

Misinterpretation of input. The input signal is clearly noted, but the meaning of the signal is misinterpreted. Systems should provide unambiguous indications of their status and the required action. Training and experience can increase the probability of correct interpretations.

Inappropriate or insufficient physical or verbal response. The user knows what to do and how to do it, but he or she takes inappropriate action. A system may require a high level of skill or physical strength to get an acceptable response. Examples of this fact are surgeons and athletes. Practicing the skill or better matching the person to the task can increase the likelihood of the appropriate response.

Lack of feedback. There is no indication that the user did the previous steps (sensing, interpreting, responding) correctly, or feedback is too vague or not timely.

Root Causes of Casualties

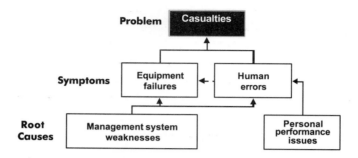

4.0 Introduction to Root Causes

Casualties are caused by combinations of equipment failure and human error. Sometimes the underlying causes result from personal performance errors; that is, all practical measures for preventing the errors had been tried. Humans will eventually make mistakes with even the most error-proofed systems. However, the underlying causes can usually be traced to weaknesses in an organization's management systems; that is, its programs and policies. These management system weaknesses lead to conditions for equipment failure and error-likely situations for individuals. These are the underlying root causes of most casualties and other unwanted situations, such as inspection deficiencies.

What is a root cause?

- Root causes are the most basic causes of an event that meet the following conditions:
    - they can be reasonably identified
    - management has the ability to fix or influence them
- Typically, root causes are the absence, neglect, or deficiencies of management systems that control human actions and equipment performance

For any event leading to a casualty, there may be more than one underlying root cause. It is not uncommon for a casualty to have many underlying root causes. If these root causes are not found and corrected, the underlying management system weaknesses will lead to casualties.

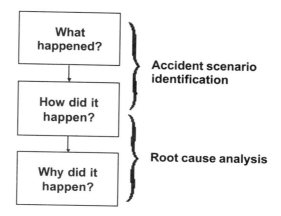

4.1 What is root cause analysis?

Root cause analysis provides a means to determine how and why something occurred. Understanding the accident scenario is not enough. Scenarios tell us what happened, not why it happened. Events in accident scenarios are generally only symptoms of underlying problems in the administrative controls that are supposed to keep those events from occurring. Understanding only the scenario addresses the outward symptoms, but not the underlying problems. More investigation of the underlying problems is needed to find and correct those that will contribute to future accidents. Root cause analysis provides a means to investigate underlying problems.

Key features of root cause analysis

- Understanding how an accident event occurred

- Discovering the underlying root causes (management system weaknesses) of the key contributors (causal factors)

- Developing and implementing practical and effective recommendations for preventing future accidents

Key differences from traditional problem solving

Logical reasoning through cause-effect relationships

Rigorous focus on factual data versus supposition

Range of possibilities considered

Management system perspective

Multiple root causes identified

Systematic processes and tools make effective data trending possible

The flowchart on the following page is modeled after the American Institute of Chemical Engineers' process for conducting incident investigations. It illustrates the complete process of performing root cause analysis.

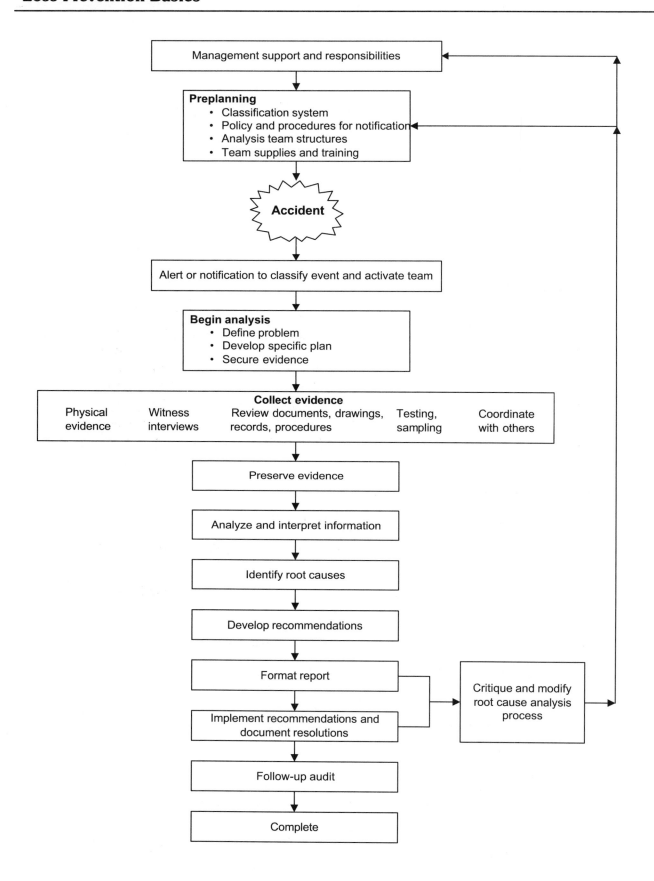

4.2 Trending analysis results

Root cause analysis results can be trended to identify persistent problem areas. Analysis teams focus on one specific event and reasonable methods for preventing recurrence. Organizations should identify systemic problems that contribute to groups of events. Trending provides the ability to associate related events.

Trending is performed by sorting various characteristics of events of interest. Trending can provide correlation of events to:

- country of operation
- division
- industry sector
- facility or vessel
- operating areas
- types of accidents
- job positions

- operating modes
- timing (seasons, days, time of day, etc.)
- environmental conditions
- contributing events
- event sequences
- root causes

Benefits of trending

Facilitates performance assessments and projections

Identifies persistent management deficiencies (root causes)

Highlights unique, unrecognized, or improperly defined risks

Identifies misallocated management resources

Flags sudden changes in performance, either positive or negative

Provides correlation of changes in performance to events producing such changes

Highlights risk assessment weaknesses

4.3 Example Root Cause Analysis Report: Investigation of the Acrylic Kettle (X-10) Incident on December 7, 1999

4.3.1 Summary of the Incident

On December 7, 1999, at approximately 11:00 p.m., the acrylic kettle (X-10) at PSI's Denver plant ruptured during production of a batch of resin (G24X104). The kettle contents were ejected, and the surrounding structures were severely damaged. The kettle operator was taken to the hospital where he recovered from second-degree burns. Small fires that were started by the materials sprayed from the kettle burned out or were quickly extinguished by plant personnel. The entire plant was shut down pending investigation of the incident and repair of the damage caused by the fire, explosion, and falling debris.

4.3.2 Incident Investigation Team

The incident investigation began on December 8, 1999, at 11:00 a.m. Larry Saunders was initially in charge of the investigation; Steve Whittle assumed responsibility for the investigation on October 6. The incident investigation team included:

Name	Title	Organization
Lee Stevens	Production Consultant	PSI Pardeville, Wisconsin
Steve Whittle	Incident Investigation Leader Senior Process Analyst	PSI Corporate
Mike Roberts	PSM Project Leader	PSI Corporate
Mike Eislie	Assistant Plant Manager	PSI Denver, Colorado
Ken Rutgers	Acrylic Unit Operator	PSI Houston, Texas
Dave Wage	PSM Project Leader	PSI Corporate
Kyle Hoops	Acrylic Unit Operator	PSI Denver, Colorado
Bill Bridges	Consultant	ABS Group Inc.
Don Lorenzo	Consultant	ABS Group Inc.
Lee Vanden Heuvel	Consultant	ABS Group Inc.

4.3.3 Investigation Methodology

The investigation team collected data concerning the incident. Data collection began on December 8,1999, and continued until December 18, 1999.

The data collected were then summarized in an Event and Causal Factors Chart (Attachment 1). This chart was used to help the investigators decide in what areas more data were necessary, and it also helps to clearly depict the relationship of key events related to the incident.

Finally, the team developed recommendations for plant management to consider. The recommendations relate to reducing or eliminating the key causal factors; therefore, addressing these recommendations should help prevent recurrence in the remaining acrylic kettle (K-25).

4.3.4 Personnel Involved in the Incident

Nick Faldo was the senior acrylics area operator working at the time of the incident. Lee Heuvel was an experienced kettle operator being trained for a new assignment in the acrylics area. He had been working in acrylics for about 7 weeks.

4.3.5 Process Description

There are two production units in adjacent buildings in the acrylics area — an older kettle (X-10) and a newer kettle (K-25), each with its own feed and product tanks. A variety of acrylic resins are produced by reacting acrylate monomers with catalysts in these kettles.

To make a batch, the desired amount of monomer is transferred from a storage tank to the monomer feed tank. Xylene solvent is pumped from storage into the kettle and the catalyst mix tank. Liquid or powdered catalyst is added to the xylene in the catalyst mix tank and blended with a small agitator. (To improve safety, production procedures were recently revised to require dilution of all catalysts with xylene; previously some catalysts had not been diluted.)

Initially, the xylene in the kettle is heated to its boiling point and refluxed through a decanter to remove any water. When the xylene is clear (water-free), the reflux is routed directly back to the kettle, bypassing the decanter. The catalyst/xylene mixture in the mix tank and the monomer in the feed tank are then pumped into the kettle at the desired rates. Steam heating through the kettle's jacket and internal half-pipe coils is maintained until the exothermic polymerization is initiated, then steam flow is stopped and cooling water is circulated.

When the batch is completed, the resin is transferred to a product tank or discharged directly to drums. The kettle is cleaned, if necessary, and the next batch is started.

4.3.6 Description of the Incident

On December 7, 1999, at approximately 5:30 p.m., the day shift began a batch of acrylic resin (G24X104) in kettle X-10 About 13,200 pounds of n-butyl acrylate monomer were pumped into the feed tank, 3,700 pounds of xylene were pumped into the kettle, and 246 pounds of xylene were pumped into the catalyst mix tank. The kettle agitator was started, and the steam valve to the kettle jacket and coil was opened to begin heating the xylene. One partial drum (204 pounds) of di-tert-butyl peroxide catalyst (DTBP) was pumped into the catalyst mix tank before shift change at 7:00 p.m.

The night shift operators, Lee Heuvel, and Nick Faldo continued work in the acrylic area. Lee, under Nick's supervision, took the lead in completing the batch in X-10 while Nick attended to drumming product from K-25 so a new batch could be started in that kettle. Lee got another DTBP catalyst drum and pumped the additional 42 pounds of catalyst needed from the drum into the catalyst mix tank. The catalyst and xylene in the catalyst mix tank should have then been agitated for 30 minutes, but this was apparently not done, either because the operator failed to start the mixer or because the mixer tripped off shortly after startup. (Lee does not specifically remember starting the agitator, but it is a routine, almost reflexive, task for an experienced operator.) Post-incident testing showed that without mechanical mixing, most of the catalyst could have remained floating as a separate liquid layer on top of the xylene in the catalyst tank. (Test also showed that catalyst and xylene are miscible and, once mixed, they do not separate.)

Meanwhile, Lee continued to prepare the kettle. The xylene in X-10 was heated to 280 °F and refluxed through the decanter to remove any water contamination that could degrade product quality (requiring filtration to remove the haze). Once the xylene was dry (about 10:00 p.m.), Nick verified the system status before Lee proceeded. Nick recalled that the catalyst mix tank agitator was off at this time, but it would have normally been shut down before feed to the kettle was started because the agitator vibration caused erratic weigh cell readings. There was no other visible indication whether the catalyst had been mixed, and Nick did not specifically question Lee about it. The valve alignment was correct, so Nick told Lee to proceed with feeding the kettle.

At about 10:05 p.m., Lee started feeding both monomer and catalyst at the desired rates. The monomer feed is relatively cool (50 °F to 60 °F), so the kettle temperature normally drops 10-15 degrees during the first 10-20 minutes of a batch. Lee correctly applied steam to the kettle jacket and internal half-pipe coils during this phase to heat the batch and initiate the exothermic reaction. (Note: It is possible that the steam flow was low despite a normal valve position [4-5 threads open], but this seems unlikely because the steam was operating normally during the earlier reflux step.) Nick checked with Lee about 10 min-utes later and verified that the reaction was proceeding normally (the temperature had dipped, steam was on, and Lee believed he saw some reflux), so Nick returned to work at K-25. The reaction, however, did not start normally because the "catalyst" being fed was probably un-mixed xylene from the bottom of the catalyst tank. Without the normal heat of reaction (or perhaps, but less likely, because of inadequate steam heat), the batch temperature continued to fall and unreacted monomer accumulated in the kettle.

The temperature dropped to 240 °F by about 10:20 p.m. before beginning to rise. At 10:55 p.m., the temperature had risen to 245 °F and Lee believed the reaction had initiated. He closed the steam valve, but the temperature promptly dropped back to 240 °F, so Lee applied more steam to the kettle to heat it back up to the normal range. When Nick checked with Lee about 11:00 p.m., he saw that the kettle temperature was abnormally low and that the steam was still on. Nick told Lee to cut back the steam flow and be ready to apply cooling water as soon as he saw any temperature rise. Nick returned to K-25.

By then, about 7,000 pounds of monomer had been fed to the kettle with the dilute xy-lene/DTBP mix-ture from the bottom of the catalyst mix tank. The concentration of DTBP in the remaining catalyst mixture was probably much higher, and it finally initiated the polymer-ization reaction as it was fed to the kettle. Lee shut off the steam and vented the kettle jacket about 3 minutes later when he saw the tem-perature had risen to 266 °F. Lee began to open the cooling water valves, but it was too late to control the runaway reaction of the unreacted monomer that had accumulated in the kettle. Xylene was vapor-ized in the kettle so fast that it overwhelmed the reflux condenser, overwhelmed the vent system, over-whelmed the pressure relief system, and overpressurized the kettle.

Shortly after 11:00 p.m., the welded joint between the kettle head and side wall failed around the entire circumference, and the head was launched upward, demolishing all the struc-ture above it. The flashing kettle contents were also ejected upward and ignited in a small fireball/explosion. The resulting pressure wave damaged surrounding structures, and debris fell in a radius of about 300 yards. Burning ejecta started several small fires around the plant, but these were quickly extinguished. Lee was hospitalized with second-degree burns; no other injuries were recorded as a result of the incident.

Contributing Factors

- Lee was a relatively new operator in the acrylics area, but he had an excellent performance record as a kettle operator in another area of the plant. He did not have enough experience with this formulation to recognize when to stop the feed streams if the batch was not progressing normally.
- Overtime had been authorized for an extra operator to stay over and train Lee. When unexpected schedule conflicts arose, no one was available to work the extra overtime as a trainer. Thus, the other operator on Lee's shift (Nick) had to divide his attention between normal work duties and training.
- The operators did not know that catalyst and xylene would not mix well unless mechanically agitated. Their perception was that mixing ensured a uniform solution and enhanced quality, but that simply pumping the two materials into the same tank would largely mix them.
- The operators had to turn off the catalyst mix tank agitator to get accurate readings from catalyst mix tank weigh cells so they could set the correct catalyst feed rate. This increased the likelihood of failing to agitate the catalyst/xylene mixture.
- The operating procedures specified only the desired temperature for the reaction. There were no safety limits stated, and no warning that feeding reactants below a certain temperature could result in accu-mulation of unreacted material and a subsequent runaway reaction when the unreacted material was heated to the catalyst activation temperature.
- The pressure relief system for the kettle was designed for a different manufacturing process. When the process was changed to produce acrylics, the relief system was not resized.

Recommendations

1. Review the design basis for the pressure relief system on the remaining acrylic kettle (K-25) to ensure that it is capable of handling a runaway reaction.
2. In the instructions for each acrylic product, specify the safe range of kettle temperatures at which monomer and catalyst may be fed.
3. Consider providing an interlock(s) to halt feed to an acrylic kettle if its temperature is outside safe limits.
4. Revise the acrylic manufacturing procedures to specify that the catalyst mixer be turned on, and have operators verify the mixer status before starting to feed monomer to the kettle.
5. Consider providing an interlock to prevent/halt monomer and catalyst feed to an acrylic kettle if the catalyst mixer is not on. (Vibration does not cause erratic readings from the weigh cells under the catalyst feed tank for K-25.)
\6. Consider providing a means for operators to see the history and trend of temperature in an acrylic kettle during a batch.
7. Specify the criteria for a qualified acrylic unit operator. What information must be known and what skills must be demonstrated before a worker is considered qualified to operate without a trainer's supervision?
8. Specify the requirements for an on-the-job trainer. What other duties is a trainer allowed to undertake while coaching a trainee?

Root Cause Analysis Results

Causal Factor	Paths Through the Root Cause Map™	Recommendation
#1 - The agitator for the catalyst mix tank was not turned on during the dilution of the catalyst with xylene, or it tripped off shortly after starting. Xylene is used to dilute the catalyst. This practice was recently started (as a result of an unrelated incident) to reduce the probability of catalyst decomposition in the feed nozzle. Xylene is pumped into the catalyst mix tank first, and catalyst is then pumped in on top of it. If the agitator for the tank is not turned on, the catalyst/xylene can stratify with the lighter di-tert-butyl peroxide (DTBP) on the top and the heavier xylene on the bottom. When the catalyst is then added to the kettle, the xylene-rich phase is added first. When the more concentrated catalyst phase is added later, the relatively large quantity of unreacted monomer that had accumulated could react more vigorously.	Procedures – Wrong/incomplete – Incomplete/situation not covered There was no step in the procedure specifying that the catalyst mix tank agitator be turned on. Immediate Supervision – Supervision during work – Supervision less than adequate (LTA) The trainee operator was required to work independently with only intermittent supervision by the qualified operator who was working overtime as a trainer. The qualified operator divided his attention between training the new operator and draining product from the adjacent kettle. Training – No training – Training requirements not identified The trainee operator was an experienced kettle operator from a different area of the plant. There were no clear performance standards to indicate when the operator had been adequately trained on the acrylic unit. Training – Training LTA – On-the-job training LTA Human Factors Engineering – Intolerant system – Errors not detectable The only indication that the mixer was on was the mixer shaft rotation. (The small motor could not be heard above other background noise.) The mixer had to be turned off so it would not interfere with the weigh cell readings during catalyst feed. There was no visual cue that the mixer had not been operated.	1. Implement a pre-startup safety review program to ensure that procedures are properly revised when changes are made and that workers are trained in the revised procedures. 2. Define the required minimum staffing of qualified operators for each shift. Prohibit the use of trainees to fill the role of a qualified operator. 3. Develop a written program for initial and refresher operator training, including specific requirements for demonstrating understanding of the training. 4. Define the expectations for qualified operators serving as on-the-job trainers. Train those operators on how to be effective trainers. 5. As part of the process hazard analysis (PHA), analyze the human-machine interface to ensure that there are adequate alarms and indications of safety-related parameters.

Root Cause Analysis Results (continued)

Causal Factor	Paths Through the Root Cause Map™	Recommendation
#2 – Hazards of inadequate catalyst mixing were not recognized. Operators were unaware that the DTBP solution was less dense than xylene and were unaware that a low catalyst concentration could exist in the bottom of the mix tank. They believed that pumping the DTBP into the xylene would largely mix the two. They were also unaware that feeding catalyst into a kettle with an accumulation of unreacted monomer could release enough energy to rupture the kettle.	Administrative/Management Systems – Standards, policies, or administrative controls (SPAC) LTA – Not strict enough	6. Revise the policy specifying the process safety information that must be transmitted to the plant, along with any formulation revisions, so management-of-change reviews can be properly performed and appropriate cautions and warnings can be incorporated into the procedures and training programs.
	Administrative/Management Systems – Safety/hazard review – Review not performed The catalyst vendor recommended diluting the catalyst to make it less reactive, and therefore safer, to add to the acrylic kettle.	7. Implement a management-of-change program to ensure that all process changes are reviewed, including those that result from incident investigations or hazard studies.
#3 – Operators failed to recognize unstable process conditions and stop kettle feeds. Temperature in the kettle decreased to 240 °F during the addition of monomer. The kettle temperature is supposed to be maintained at 270-285 °F during the addition of monomer. Monomer addition causes the kettle temperature to decrease because it is relatively cold (typically 55-65 °F). Kettle temperature is maintained by controlling steam flow to the kettle. Kettle steam flow was only partially on.	Procedures – Wrong/incomplete – Situation not covered Operators indicated that they had general guidelines for maintaining the kettle temperature while adding monomer. However, there were no safe limits specified for this system and no clear guidance for actions to be taken when the temperature fell outside these bounds.	8. Develop safe operating limits for process parameters and state them in the procedures. Include procedural instructions on how to respond if operating limits are exceeded.
The qualified operator failed to recognize that continuing to feed monomer while the kettle temperature was too low could lead to an uncontrollable runaway reaction. The digital temperature indication gave no indication of the reaction history.	Training – Training LTA – Abnormal events/emergency training LTA Operators did not realize the severe consequences associated with accumulating unreacted monomer in the kettle. The operator was more concerned about overheating the kettle and did not add more steam quickly to initiate the reaction.	9. Train operators in recognizing potential upsets and in the proper corrective action. Emphasize that stopping feed to exothermic reactions is a preferred option, not a last resort.
	Administrative/Management Systems – Safety/hazard review – Review not performed The PHA was not performed because the unit was scheduled for shutdown 2 years ago. A PHA team may have identified this accident scenario and recommended additional or revised safeguards.	10. Develop complete process safety information, including reaction kinetics, for each formulation manufactured and update all PHAs based on this information.

Root Cause Analysis Results (continued)

Causal Factor	Paths Through the Root Cause Map™	Recommendation
#3 – (continued)	**Administrative/Management Systems** – SPAC LTA – No SPAC Previous events occurred where the kettle temperature and pressure had fallen outside the acceptable range. In at least one previous event, the temperature had reached 350 °F (the acceptable range was 270-285 °F), and pressure had reached 20-25 psig (the acceptable range is -3 to +3 psig). Had that incident been reported/investigated, the procedures and training might have been revised and this incident avoided.	11. Develop a program for investigating near misses as well as incidents.
	Human Factors Engineering – Workplace layout – Displays LTA The system did not provide the information needed by the operator. The digital temperature indication does not provide any trend information that the operator can use to see whether the batch temperature is behaving normally.	12. As part of the PHA, analyze the human-machine interface to ensure that there are adequate alarms and indications of safety-related parameters.
#4 – The kettle pressure relief system appears to be undersized. As pressure in the kettle increased, the relief system was unable to adequately relieve the pressure. The pressure relief system consists of a rupture disk upstream of a relief valve.	**Administrative/Management Systems** – Document and configuration control – Control of official documents LTA There was no documentation of the design basis for the pressure relief system.	13. Develop a data management system for process safety information, including the design bases for pressure relief devices and ventilation systems, for all process equipment.
The pressure relief line appears to be undersized. The relief valve was a 1.5 × 2-inch valve. The new acrylic kettle (K-25) has an 8-inch rupture disk relieving to atmosphere in addition to a 1.5 × 2-inch valve.	**Administrative/Management Systems** – Safety/hazard review – Review not performed The kettle was used to make epoxies about 5 years ago before it was changed to make acrylics. There is no record that the hazards associated with the change were reviewed or that the relief system sizing was reevaluated.	14. Implement a management-of-change program to ensure that all process changes are reviewed and that the process safety information is updated to reflect those changes 15. Develop a policy specifying the information that must be transmitted to the plant, along with any new formulations, so management-of-change reviews can be properly performed.
	Design Input/Output – Design input LTA – Design input not correct A previous manager decided that external fire was the maximum credible design basis for kettle pressure relief systems. There was no evaluation of other, potentially more demanding, design bases for the pressure relief system.	16. In the process safety information, document that all equipment conforms to good engineering practice (i.e., conforms to current codes and standards) or document the analysis concluding that the equipment is safe for continued use in its current application (even if it does not conform to current codes and practice).

Root Cause Analysis Results (continued)

Causal Factor	Paths Through the Root Cause Map™	Recommendation
#5 – The kettle appears to have failed below its design burst pressure. Visual inspection of the kettle top (which was blown off the kettle and landed approximately 50 feet from the kettle) indicates that much of the fracture occurred previously. Some areas of the break are shiny, indicating that the break occurred recently; other areas of the break show significant oxidation, indicating that there was an existing crack in that area.	Inspection/Testing Program – Inspection/testing program LTA – Routine testing program LTA The kettle was normally operated near atmospheric pressure and was slated for decommissioning, so vessel inspections were given low priority. Records of the last inspection could not be located. Administrative/Management Systems – Corrective action – Corrective action LTA Operator observation of "weeping" from the weld joint indicated that the weld integrity was suspect, but no corrective action was taken.	17. Develop a mechanical integrity program to ensure that equipment is fit for its intended use over the life of the facility. Ensure that equipment records are kept current. 18. Ensure that deficient equipment is repaired, derated, or removed from service when tests or inspections indicate a deficiency.
#6 – Emergency response was delayed. (Not shown on causal factor chart) After the incident, the emergency response was delayed because the operators could not get through to 911 and because no one on site had a key to the main gate.	Communications – No communication or not timely – No method available Training – Training LTA – Abnormal events/emergency training LTA	19. Provide a more reliable means to summon outside responders in an emergency. 20. Exercise the emergency response plan periodically to ensure that it will be effective on all shifts. Revise the plan as necessary and train personnel in their proper roles.

Shift Change 7:00 PM

Top timeline events (left to right):

Source	Event/Action	Time
Ken	Ken started batch of G24X104 about 5:30 - 6:00pm	
Ken	Charged monomer to feed tank (Butyl Acrylate) 13,200#	
Ken	Charged xylene to catalyst mix tank (246#) and to kettle (3700#)	
Ken	Opened steam valve 4-5 turns to slowly heat kettle and xylene	
Ken	Turned on kettle agitator (83-85 rpm)	6:30
Ken	On second floor, began charging di-tert-butyl-peroxide to catalyst mix tank (partial drum emptied at 204 lb)	6:35
Ken	Got another partial drum of catalyst and left it downstairs	
Ken	Told Nick and Lee to add 42# to catalyst mix tank to finish charge	
Lee	Lee moved catalyst drum upstairs (about 15 min)	
Lee	Charged 42# of catalyst to mix tank (about 15 min)	
Lee	Switched reflux return from kettle to decanter to collect water	7:30
Nick	Lee changed reflux return from decanter to kettle	10:00
Nick	Nick visually verified vent valve position (opened) and went to clean filter of other kettle (K-25)	

Conditions (shaded, above events):

Source	Condition
Lee	Kettle temperature was 170 °F
Lee	Kettle temperature was 280 °F and reflux was hazy
Lee	Kettle temperature was 280 °F and reflux was clear (no water present)

Connector A (right side continuation)

Below events:

This was first batch of G24X104 with the catalyst diluted with xylene

CF #1

Catalyst mix tank agitator not turned on or tripped off (normally turned on when fully charged). Operator can't remember if it was turned on

Source	Condition
All Operators	Typically catalyst is agitated for 30 minutes in mix tank
Paper	No step for this in procedure
All Employees	Trainee performed procedure

Connector B:

| Nick | Catalyst agitator was off and no indication that agitator had/had not been operated |

CF #2

| All Operators | Operators unaware of hazards of inadequate catalyst mixing |

Legend

Source

Fact

Assumption or Conclusion

Time

Shade ☐ = Condition
Unshaded ☐ = Event/Action
CF = Causal Factor

Attachment 1 Event and Causal Factors Chart

References

EQE International, Inc. *Root Cause Analysis Handbook: A Guide to Effective Incident Investigation.* Rockville: ABS Consulting/Government Institutes, 1999.

Chapter 3
Principles of Risk Assessment

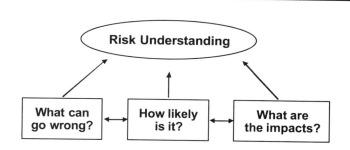

1.0 Characterizing Risk

Understanding risk requires answers to the following questions:

What can go wrong?

Risk assessment methods are used to identify combinations of events that can create casualties. These can include equipment failures, human errors, and external events. Based on the quantity and types of events that may occur, an analyst gains a good understanding of the risk associated with an issue of concern.

How likely is it?

Likelihood is usually expressed as the probability or frequency of an accident occurring. If the likelihood is low enough, analysts may conclude that a possible accident scenario is not credible, not of concern, or of extremely low risk. But, the criteria for making such judgments often change with the type and severity of the consequence related to the possible accident.

What are the impacts?

An accident can affect many areas of concern with different degrees of negative results. However, this accident may not cause environmental damage or public injury. The type and severity of consequences related to an accident help an analyst understand and judge risk.

Elements of risk

Frequency   Consequence

- **Risk is the combination of frequency (F) and consequence (C), often expressed as F x C**
- **Two categories of risk**
  - ◆ **risks that can be reduced or eliminated**
  - ◆ **remaining risks**

1.1 Elements of risk

Frequency. The frequency of events is often expressed as *events per year.* However, other bases for expressing how frequently an event will occur are also used. These include *events per mile traveled, events per transit, events per ton of material moved, etc.*

The frequency should be determined from past data if a large number of events have occurred. However, we usually focus on accidents with severe consequences for which few data records exist. For these events, frequency is calculated using risk assessment models.

The frequency of any event is based on (1) how often the hazard is present (*i.e.,* how many times an operation is performed) and (2) the probability of experiencing the accident during any exposure to the hazard. Some descriptions of risk will explicitly describe frequency as the number of exposures to the hazard, multiplied by the probability of an accident during each exposure.

Consequence. Consequence is measured by the magnitude of its effects. Consequence is expressed as the number of people injured or killed, area affected, outage time, mission delay, dollars lost, etc.

Risk. The risk of a potential accident is often calculated as the combination of the frequency and consequence. This way, we can compare the risks of different operations and potential accidents. However, you should also compare the two *consequences,* because we often judge risk with a higher priority given to high-consequence events.

For example, suppose Potential Accident #1 has a frequency of once in 100 years and a consequence of $10,000. Potential Accident #2 has a frequency of once in 10,000 years and a consequence of $1 million. The risk of either potential accident is $100/yr ($10,000 x 1/100 yr or $1 million x 1/10,000 yr), but you might be more concerned about Potential Accident #2 than Potential Accident #1 based on the severity of the consequence.

Risk acceptance criteria. Any operation has risks. Once these risks are known, we can take steps to reduce them (e.g., insulate hot surfaces to reduce the chance of getting burned) or eliminate them (e.g., switching to nonflammable cleaning materials to eliminate a fire hazard). However, some known risks are accepted as the *cost of doing business*. These remaining risks, known as residual risks, should be within an organization's risk acceptance criteria.

Risk characterization methods

- **Quantitative**
  - **point risk estimate**
  - **categorization**
  - **probability distributions**
- **Qualitative**
  - **subjective prioritization**
  - **basic scenario ranking**
  - **criteria-based scenario ranking**

1.2 Risk characterization methods

Risk assessment involves processing a large quantity of data: Often hundreds or even thousands of accident scenarios must be evaluated to estimate the risk of an operation. An analyst should consider the level of detail needed in the risk results before starting the risk assessment process. Qualitative methods, as well as coarse and detailed quantitative methods, can characterize risk. Qualitative methods may suffice when focusing on the *big picture* and identifying general operations where higher risk exists. However, in other situations, a more detailed risk assessment is needed.

1.2.1 Quantitative risk characterization

Quantitative risk characterization methods provide decision makers with precise descriptions of risk; however, these methods often involve detailed studies that are very resource intensive. Also, be careful not to confuse precise descriptions of risk with the accuracy or certainty of those descriptions. Applying quantitative risk characterization methods generally requires a substantial level of experience and expertise among analysis team members. Two common forms of quantitative risk characterization are the following:

Point risk estimates. An analysis team uses historical data from directly related operational experience, expert judgment, and data published from other applications of similar equipment or human activities to estimate (1) the frequency of initiating events for various accident scenarios and (2) the probability of failure for each safeguard. The effect of the consequence, often measured in cost or injuries and deaths, is also estimated.

Categorizations. A risk assessment team assigns accident scenarios to appropriate likelihood and consequence categories. The combination of likelihood and consequence category is used to assign a risk level to the scenario.

Probability distributions. A risk assessment team assigns probability distributions to reflect the possible range of event frequencies, probabilities, and consequences that may be applicable for a specific assessment. This method is more robust than simply selecting point estimates as described above because the uncertainty associated with each key frequency, probability, or consequence number is modeled. However, this method is considerably more complicated to apply and will not be discussed further in these *Principles*.

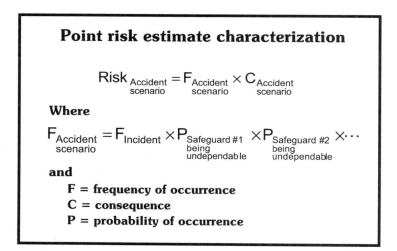

Point risk estimate characterization

$$\text{Risk}_{\substack{\text{Accident} \\ \text{scenario}}} = F_{\substack{\text{Accident} \\ \text{scenario}}} \times C_{\substack{\text{Accident} \\ \text{scenario}}}$$

Where

$$F_{\substack{\text{Accident} \\ \text{scenario}}} = F_{\text{Incident}} \times P_{\substack{\text{Safeguard \#1} \\ \text{being} \\ \text{undependable}}} \times P_{\substack{\text{Safeguard \#2} \\ \text{being} \\ \text{undependable}}} \times \cdots$$

and

    F = frequency of occurrence
    C = consequence
    P = probability of occurrence

1.2.2 Point risk estimate characterization

Point estimates of risk provide decision makers with very precise information about the absolute magnitude of risk associated with specific activities. These precise estimates are particularly useful when decisions will be sensitive to small, subtle differences in risk.

Example for oil spill scenarios

Scenarios	Incident	Failed Safeguards		Scenario Frequencies
Scenario 1	Valve leaks (1/y)	Flow not stopped x (0.1) x	Oil enters water (0.01)	= 0.001/y
Scenario 2	Hose leaks (0.1/y)	Flow not stopped x (0.1) x	Oil enters water (0.1)	= 0.001/y
Scenario 3	Hose ruptures (0.01/y)	Flow not stopped x (1.0)	Oil enters water (1.0)	= 0.01/y
			$F_{accident}$ =	0.012/y

Risk = 0.012/y x $10,000 = $120/y

As you can see from the table above, three different scenarios have been identified that could cause the same accident, which has an associated consequence of $10,000. The accident frequency is the sum of the scenario frequencies. Knowing the accident frequency, consequence, and risk, management can now determine if the accident risk is acceptable. If not, these same results help us focus on areas where additional control efforts may be needed.

Limitations of point risk estimate

- Accuracy depends on accuracy and completeness of scenario models and specific likelihood and consequence data for each event

- Very resource intensive for detailed studies

- Point estimate choices are often based on subjective choices

---

> ### Risk characterization using categorization
>
> - Can provide most types of risk-based information
> - Generally efficient to apply
> - Often an excellent screening approach

1.2.3 Risk characterization using categorization

The risk assessment process changes very little if risk is to be characterized using categories instead of point estimates. In this case, the analyst must (1) define the likelihood and consequence categories to be used in evaluating accident scenario risk acceptability and (2) define the level of risk associated with each likelihood and consequence category combination. In defining categories, be careful to provide enough so that meaningful results are ob-tained, but not so many that risk assessment teams have difficulty assigning category values to scenarios.

For example, using too few categories may cause analysts to assign all the accident scenarios to the same risk level. In this case, very little is learned in the risk assessment process and no direction is given as to where to focus management controls. Too many categories, on the other hand, will consume excessive amounts of the risk assessment team's time in determining the *right* category assignment for each accident scenario.

Frequency and consequence categories

The following tables are the basis for a scenario-based risk categorization system. Multiple consequence classification criteria may be required to address safety, environmental, operability, and other types of consequences.

Example criteria for consequences

This table is an example of a scheme for estimating the effects of a specific accident scenario. The most applicable category would be chosen for the scenario using the definitions provided.

Example Types of Effects*				
Severity	Safety Impact	Environmental Impact	Economic Impact	Mission Impact
Major (1)	One or more deaths or permanent disability	Releases that result in long-term disruption of the ecosystem or long-term exposure to chronic health risks	≥ $3M	≥ $3M
Moderate (2)	Injury that requires hospitalization or lost work days	Releases that result in short-term disruption of the ecosystem	≥$10K and <$3M	≥$10K and <$3M
Minor (3)	Injury that requires first aid	Pollution with minimal acute environmental or public health impact	≥ $100 and <$10K	≥ $100 and <$10K

* Losses in these categories result from both immediate and long-term effects (e.g., considering both acute and chronic effects when evaluating safety and health).

Example criteria for frequency

This table is an example of a scheme for scoring frequencies of accident scenarios. The most applicable score would be chosen for each scenario using the descriptions provided.

Frequency Category	Description
Very Frequent	From 10 to 100 events per year in the port
Frequent	From 1 to 10 events per year in the port
Occasional	From 1 event every 10 years to 1 event per year in the port
Infrequent	Less than 1 event every 10 years in the port
Rare	Not expected to occur in the port

Example risk matrix

The following matrix provides a mechanism for assigning risk, and making risk acceptance decisions, using a risk categorization approach. Each cell in the matrix corresponds to a specific combination of likelihood and consequence. Thus, each cell indicates the risk of a scenario having that combination of likelihood and consequence. Each cell in the matrix can be assigned a priority number or some other risk descriptor, as shown in the matrix below. An organization must define the categories it will use to score risks and, more importantly, how it will prioritize and respond to the various levels of risk associated with cells in the matrix.

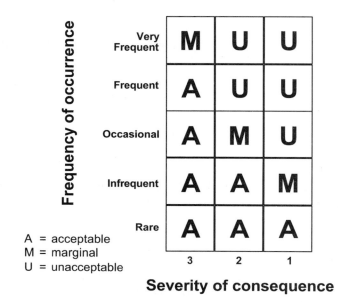

A = acceptable
M = marginal
U = unacceptable

Severity of consequence

Example Risk Acceptability Matrix

Scenario	Frequency and Severity Estimates			Risk Acceptability
	Level 3 Severity	Level 2 Severity	Level 1 Severity	
Scenario 1	Very frequent (Risk: M)	Infrequent (Risk: A)	Rare (Risk: A)	M
Scenario 2	Occasional (Risk: A)	Occasional (Risk: M)	Infrequent (Risk: M)	M
Scenario 3	Frequent (Risk: A)	Infrequent (Risk: A)	Rare (Risk: A)	A

Example loss estimates

The significance of a risk matrix can be further understood by generating the estimated losses associated with it. In the table below, the risk assessment team estimated how often each scenario will occur and how often it will result in consequences in each of these severity levels. For example, the team determined that Scenario #3 will result in a Level 3 severity 1 to 10 times per year and essentially never result in a Level 1 severity. You can add the ranges of the frequency estimates for all scenarios to determine the Frequency Summary of each severity level. To get the range of Expected Losses for each severity level, multiply the upper and lower bounds of the Frequency Summary with the average consequence for the severity level. The total expected range of annual losses presented below the table is the sum of the Expected Losses for all severity levels.

Example Loss Estimates

Scenario	Frequency and Severity Estimates		
	3 ($100 to $10K) Average Consequence: $3K	2 ($10K to $3M) Average Consequence: $300K	1 (>$3M) Average Consequence: $5M
Scenario #1	Very Frequent 10/yr to 100/yr	Infrequent 0/yr to 0.1/yr	Rare 0/yr
Scenario #2	Occasional 0.1/yr to 1/yr	Occasional 0.1/yr to 1/yr	Infrequent 0/yr to 0.1/yr
Scenario #3	Frequent 1/yr to 10/yr	Infrequent 0/yr to 0.1/yr	Rare 0/yr
Frequency Summary (by Severity Level)	11.1/yr to 111/yr	0.1/yr to 1.2/yr	0/yr to 0.1/yr
Expected Losses (by Severity Level)	Using the Average Consequence: ~$33K/yr to $333K/yr	Using the Average Consequence: ~$30K/yr to $360K/yr	Using the Average Consequence: ~$0K/yr to $500K/yr

Total Expected Annual Losses: ~$63K/yr to ~$1.2M/yr

Limitations of risk characterization using categorization

- Less precise than point estimates
- Accuracy depends on
  - accuracy of scenario models
  - judgment and experience of those assigning scores for scenarios
  - quality of available scenario data
- Results are often subjective, especially for rare scenarios

> **Qualitative risk characterization**
>
> - Subjective prioritization
> - Basic scenario ranking
> - Criteria-based scenario ranking

1.2.4 Qualitative risk characterization

As you would expect, qualitative methods are easier and faster to use in characterizing risk than quantitative methods. These methods generally require less experience and expertise among risk assessment team members as well.

Subjective prioritization — A risk assessment team assigns accident scenario risk (i.e., priority) based on its collective judgment of the likelihood and severity of the failures involved in the scenario

Basic scenario ranking — A risk assessment team assigns points to each failure in a accident scenario based on the type of each failure. The points are summed to get the scenario risk. Higher scores indicate lower risks because more failures, or failures of more reliable safeguards, are required to complete the sequence.

Criteria-based scenario ranking — A risk assessment team determines if accident scenario risk is acceptable or unacceptable based on the number and type of failures described in the accident scenario. Scenarios with unacceptable risks are subject to further control measures.

> **Subjective prioritization**
>
> - Identify potential accident scenarios using structured hazard assessment techniques
> - Subjectively categorize scenarios according to their perceived level of risk

1.2.5 Subjective prioritization

Subjective prioritization identifies potential accident scenarios using structured hazard assessment techniques. This technique subjectively assigns each scenario to a priority category based on the perceived level of risk. Priority categories can be the following:

- low, medium, high
- numerical assignments
- priority levels

Of course, the results from this technique are highly dependent on the experience of the team performing the prioritization.

Example of subjective prioritization of 20 scenarios:

- **Priority 1** ➡ **Scenarios 3, 7, 15**

- **Priority 2** ➡ **Scenarios 1, 5, 16, 18, 19**

- **Priority 3** ➡ **Scenarios 2, 4, 6, 8, 9, 10, 11, 12, 13, 14, 17, 20**

Limitations of subjective prioritization

- Very subjective: Results are highly dependent on the analyst's perception of risk

- Provides only general prioritization of scenarios

- Provides limited direction to management on where to focus control efforts

---

Basic scenario ranking

- Identify potential accident scenarios
- Score scenarios based on types and numbers of events
- Prioritize based on scores

1.2.6 Basic scenario ranking

The basic scenario ranking technique allows an analyst to systematically prioritize various accident scenarios of interest. Scores are assigned to each failure in an accident scenario, and the values are totaled to yield a scenario risk score. Similarly, the risk scores for all scenarios that have the same outcome can be totaled to estimate risk. Thus, this method allows analysts to screen various types of accidents as well as scenarios that contribute to accidents.

Limitations of basic scenario ranking

- Provides only general prioritization of scenarios
- Basis of scoring has inherent limitations and inaccuracies

> ## Criteria-based scenario evaluation
>
> - **Derived from the basic scenario ranking method**
> - **Efficient to implement**
> - **Effective screening tool**

1.2.7 Criteria-based scenario evaluation

The criteria-based ranking is a derivative of the basic scenario ranking method. The two key differences are that numerical scores are not used and the scenario risk results are binary (i.e., pass or fail). Specific recommendations are made based on failure to meet the acceptance criteria.

Preestablished criteria

Preestablished criteria are listed in the table below. The left-hand column of this table shows the type of evaluation criteria illustrated by the actual criteria in the right-hand column. The specific scenario can now be evaluated based on how well it meets these specific preestablished criteria.

Type of Criteria	Examples
Number of safeguards that must fail before a specific accident of interest occurs (i.e., the number of events in each scenario)	There may not be any one-event scenarios capable of causing a major explosion in an engine room
Types of safeguards that must fail before a specific accident of interest occurs (i.e., the types of events in each scenario)	There may not be a situation in which a high pressure excursion in a boiler could occur without at least one equipment failure in addition to the equipment failure or human error that initiated the high pressure (i.e., no complete dependence on human response to the upset condition) An active and a passive equipment protection, or two passive equipment protections, are required for any scenario capable of causing a catastrophic consequence
Combinations of the number and types of safeguards that must fail before a specific accident of interest occurs (i.e., the numbers and types of events in each scenario)	Single-event scenarios are only acceptable if the event is a passive equipment failure **and** the worst-case effect would not be catastrophic Scenarios involving multiple passive equipment failures are considered practically impossible unless there is some dependency (i.e., common cause) between the failures

Limitations of criteria-based scenario evaluation

• Basis of criteria has inherent limitations and inaccuracies

1.3 Risk reduction methods

As presented earlier in this section, risk assessment involves processing a large quantity of data to characterize the risk of a system or activity. The next step is understanding what changes will reduce the risk to acceptable levels. Point estimates and categorization methods can be used to assess the impact of change.

Point estimates. Point estimates provide precise calculations of the risk associated with a particular activity. When recommending change, the same point estimate process can be applied to the activity, considering the frequency of initiating events and the failure of safeguards both before and after the proposed change. Comparing the point estimates after the change to those before provides an assessment of the impact of the change.

Categorization. Using likelihood and consequence categories, the outcomes of each applicable scenario are evaluated both before and after the change. Results are generally presented in a tabular or matrix form to provide the analyst with an overall assessment of the change for all affected scenarios.

Example risk reduction using categorization

Using risk categories (i.e., categories for frequency and severity) to assess change is an *effective* means for getting a high-level view of the overall risk associated with a system or activity and provides the analyst with a framework for recommending change. In the risk matrix below, the numbers in each box represent the number of scenarios that have the associated frequency and severity pairs. For example, when analyzing a particular piece of equipment, the team identified 175 scenarios having an "Occasional" frequency with a "C" severity. Similarly, the team identified four scenarios having a "Frequent" frequency with a "B" severity.

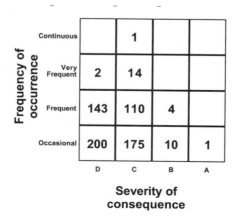

Frequency of occurrence	D	C	B	A
Continuous		1		
Very Frequent	2	14		
Frequent	143	110	4	
Occasional	200	175	10	1

Severity of consequence

These types of risk matrices can be used in two ways: (1) to assess where the risks are in a system or activity and thus identify what areas should be considered for change, and (2) to illustrate the impact of change by showing how the numbers shift to other regions in the matrix.

After recommending change to a system, the team revisited the affected scenarios and reassessed the associated frequency and severity categories. The following matrix illustrates the results.

After Implementing Changes to Reduce Risk

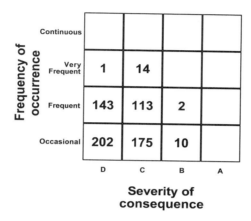

As shown, both of the single high-risk events (i.e., the event with the high frequency and the event with the catastrophic severity) as well as some of the lower-risk issues have been reduced to lower risk categories. This revised matrix illustrates the new characterization of the risk as a result of the changes.

Once the "before" and "after" risk matrices are developed, the risk reduction impact can be determined. The following two tables show the same "before" and "after" risk matrices slightly reconfigured to aid in determining the estimated impact of the changes to the system.

Both tables summarize the frequency and severity of all loss scenarios evaluated in an analysis. For example, in the first table the team determined that there were 143 loss scenarios that could result in Level D losses 1 to 10 times per year. Next, multiply the 143 scenarios by their associated frequency range of 1/yr to 10/yr (giving 143 to 1,430 losses per year). Do the same for the rest of the scenarios under Level D and sum the results to determine the Frequency Summary of Level D losses. You can determine the Frequency Summary for the other three severity levels the same way. To get the range of Expected Losses for each severity level, multiply the upper and lower bounds of the Frequency Summary with the average consequence for the severity level. The total expected range of annual losses presented below the table is the sum of the Expected Losses for all severity levels.

Before Implementing Changes to Reduce Risk

Example Loss Estimates

Frequency	Severity Level			
	D ($1K to $10K) Average Consequence: $1K	**C** ($10K to $100K) Average Consequence: $30K	**B** ($100K to $1M) Average Consequence: $300K	**A** ($1M to $10M) Average Consequence: $3M
Continuous (Between 100 events every year and 1,000 events every year)		1		
Very Frequent (Between 10 events every year and 100 events every year)	2	14		
Frequent (Between 1 event every year and 10 events every year)	143	110	4	
Occasional (Between 1 event every 10 years and 1 event every year)	200	175	10	1
Frequency Summary (by Severity Level)	183 to 1,830 per year	367.5 to 3,675 per year	5 to 50 per year	0.1 to 1 per year
Expected Losses (by Severity Level)	Using the Average Consequence: $183K to $1.83M per year	Using the Average Consequence: $11.025M to $110.25M per year	Using the Average Consequence: $1.5M to $15M per year	Using the Average Consequence: $300K to $3M per year

Total Expected Annual Losses: $13.008M to $130.08M

After Implementing Changes to Reduce Risk

Example Loss Estimates

Frequency	Severity Level			
	D ($1K to $10K) Average Consequence: $1K	**C** ($10K to $100K) Average Consequence: $30K	**B** ($100K to $1M) Average Consequence: $300K	**A** ($1M to $10M) Average Consequence: $3M
Continuous (Between 100 events every year and 1,000 events every year)				
Very Frequent (Between 10 events every year and 100 events every year)	1	14		
Frequent (Between 1 event every year and 10 events every year)	143	113	2	
Occasional (Between 1 event every 10 years and 1 event every year)	202	175	10	
Frequency Summary (by Severity Level)	173.2 to 1,732 per year	270.5 to 2,705 per year	3 to 30 per year	Level A losses are not expected to occur
Expected Losses (by Severity Level)	Using the Average Consequence: $173K to $1.73M per year	Using the Average Consequence: $8.115M to $81.15M per year	Using the Average Consequence: $900K to $9M per year	Level A losses are not expected to occur

Total Expected Annual Losses: $9.188M to $91.88M

The expected risk reduction after the recommended changes are made is the difference in the Total Expected Annual Losses between these two tables. In this example, the expected risk reduction is between $3.82M and $38.2M.

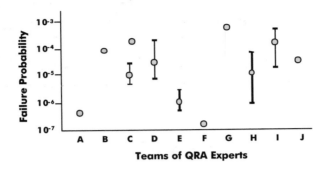

Influence of assumptions

1.4 Influence of assumptions

When performing risk assessments, you should pay attention to any assumptions made when identifying accidents and estimating accident likelihoods and consequences. The above graph shows the results of a study in which several teams of risk experts calculated the failure probability of a system. The circles represent each team's estimated failure probability, and the bars show the uncertainty bands that some teams developed with their estimates. All the experts were given the same system design and the same failure data for the system components. The different answers were attributed to the different assumptions the experts made. When the study was repeated with the same assumptions, each team produced similar answers.

Involving the right group of stakeholders, not just one subject matter expert, and building consensus about assumptions and scope limitations will help you avoid similar problems in your own risk assessments.

> **Risk Assessment**
>
> **Many risk assessment methods exist; however, they have common features:**
> - structured
> - predictive
> - experience based
> - adaptive

2.0 Introduction to Risk Assessment Methods

There are many risk assessment methods. No one is inherently better or worse than another. They all have appropriate applications and share the following features:

Structured. Each risk assessment method has some type of structure to promote a complete examination of possible problems. Some methods have very rigid structures, while others are more flexible. More highly structured methods usually provide a more complete evaluation, but they often require much more analysis effort. Although less structured risk assessment methods require less skill to apply, they need more input from subject matter experts to make up for issues that the basic nature of the assessment might overlook.

Predictive. Some risk assessment methods can be valuable for investigating accidents that do occur. However, the main use of such methods is to characterize the possibility of future accidents. Therefore, risk assessment forecasts what is expected in the future.

Experience based. Risk assessments are predictive, but they do not ignore the past. Some of the best insight into possible accidents is based on information about the types, frequencies, and severities of past accidents in the same or similar operations. Risk assessments use this information, as well as information about corrective actions taken to address past accidents, to examine expected performance. Risk assessment methods gather this information from many sources, including records (equipment files, maintenance records, electronic databases, manufacturer information, etc.) and the opinions of subject matter experts (experienced engineers, operators, technicians, and others).

Adaptive. Most risk assessment methods can be used at various levels of detail and for many types of systems and processes. This adaptive nature makes most risk assessment methods very flexible.

> **Information available from risk assessments**
>
> - Qualitative accident scenario descriptions
> - Qualitative judgments about expected accidents
> - Quantitative measures of factors related to loss prevention
> - Importance of accident contributors
> - Recommendations for improvement

2.1 Information available from risk assessments

The information produced from risk assessments can be divided into the following categories:

Qualitative accident scenario descriptions. These descriptions define sequences of events capable of producing accidents of interest. The sequences can include equipment failures, human errors, and external influences.

Example:

- Carpenter or painter fails to wear appropriate eye protection and is injured from flying debris.

Qualitative judgments about expected accidents. Analysts often have informed opinions about whether the threat of possible accidents will exceed stated or implied loss prevention goals. These judgments are usually based on the numbers and types of events possibly leading to accidents. Judgments regarding the numbers of events would look at such things as single failures or errors versus multiple-event scenarios. Judgments regarding types of events would look at such things as equipment failures while in service, equipment failures in stand-by safety systems, mistakes made by forgetting to do something, mistakes made by doing the wrong thing, etc. These judgments are often made based on decisions made in other studies.

Example:

- The frequency and severity of injuries from personnel coming into contact with flying debris in the facility will be much less when personnel are required to wear safety glasses.

Quantitative measures of factors related to loss prevention. These numeric estimates of loss prevention-related factors include measures such as reliability, availability, environmental risk, personnel or public risk, economic risk, etc. The measures are used to judge whether the threat of possible accidents exceeds numerical loss prevention goals. Sometimes these measures include studies (*what-if* scenarios) of sensitivity to changes such as implementation of recommendations, changes in operating conditions or strategies, etc.

Example:

- We expect that between one and 10 people will sustain temporarily disabling injuries leading to four or more days of lost time per person each year.

Importance of accident contributors. These results show the most important possible accidents based upon the likelihood and consequences of those accidents. Importance rankings can prioritize not only types of accidents, but also specific equipment failures and human errors.

Example:

- Failure to wear safety glasses and other personal protective equipment contributes to personnel injury at facilities in 50% of the identified accidents. Excessive lifting contributes to personnel injury in 35% of the accidents. The top contributors associated with the remaining 15% of the accidents are evenly divided between fatigue and automobile accidents.

Recommendations for improvement. Typical risk assessment results also include suggestions for reducing the frequency of accidents or preventing them altogether. These recommendations include suggestions for new or improved engineered systems, programs, policies, and items for further study. These recommendations may lessen the likelihood or consequences of an accident.

Example:

- Consider requiring personnel to wear hearing protection while using power tools such as saws and sanders. Consider enrolling these people in the formal hearing conservation program.

```
┌─────────────────────────────────────────────┐
│          Life cycle approach to               │
│        performing risk assessments            │
│                                                │
│   ■ Research           ■ Operation             │
│   ■ Design                ◆ startup            │
│      ◆ conceptual         ◆ ongoing            │
│      ◆ preliminary     ■ Decommissioning       │
│      ◆ detailed                                │
│   ■ Fabrication/                               │
│     construction/                              │
│     manufacturing                              │
└─────────────────────────────────────────────┘
```

2.2 Life cycle approach to performing risk assessments

Risk assessments can be used at *every* step in the life cycle of a system or process. The following sections discuss the use of risk assessment throughout a life cycle.

Research. Risk assessment focus at this stage is on identifying the safety and reliability of certain technologies. Assessments are performed using technical models to help us understand how failures occur over time.

Design. Risk assessment focus at this stage is on making sure that the selected operating strategy will meet overall goals. Risk managers are very interested in identifying *weak links* and opportunities for improvement in components and systems.

- **Conceptual phase.** Risk assessment focus at this stage is on deciding how overall goals can be used to define goals for individual systems. Without reviewing a lot of detail, assessments consider whether or not the system will be able to perform as expected and what changes or improvements would be needed to meet overall goals. Risk managers compare different design ideas to decide which options make the most sense based on several factors, including project risk and expected life cycle costs such as the cost of accidents and their prevention.

- **Preliminary phase.** Risk assessment focus at this stage is on how individual system goals can be used to define component goals. Assessments consider at a more detailed level whether or not the system will be able to perform as expected and what changes or improvements would be needed to meet system goals. The most favorable system performance features are based on a number of factors, including costs, loss of commerce, risk, etc.

- **Detailed phase.** Risk assessment focus at this stage is on making sure the selected components work together so that the systems can meet individual component goals. Assessments consider at a component level whether or not the components will be able to perform as expected and what changes or improvements would be needed to meet component goals. The most effective component selection is based on a number of factors, including costs, loss of commerce, risk, etc. Risk managers are also interested in the following:

  - critical limits for safe and reliable fabrication, construction, and manufacturing
  - important operating limits and startup guidelines
  - appropriate preventive or predictive maintenance jobs
  - necessary spare parts and materials stores

Fabrication, construction, and manufacturing. Risk assessment focus at this stage is on making sure that specifications have been met. The assessment also tries to find any fabrication, construction, and manufacturing issues that could negatively affect the system, leading to loss. Assessments consider the importance of any identified field defects, as well as any suggested changes during fabrication, construction, and manufacturing.

Operation. Risk assessment focus at this stage is on the effectiveness of operating, maintenance, and supply strategies for reaching loss prevention goals.

- **Startup.** Risk assessment focus at this stage is on making sure that operating and maintenance plans (including programs, procedures, and training) help to achieve the safety and reliability designed into the system and are effective based on factors including costs, loss of mission, risk, etc.

- **Ongoing.** Analysis focus at this stage is on ensuring the following:

  - changes (planned, unplanned, and unintentional) do not greatly affect loss prevention performance
  - operating and maintenance plans are effective based on several factors, including costs, loss of commerce, risk, etc.

Decommissioning. Risk assessment focus at this stage is on liability issues related to removing equipment from service and what actions to take to make sure those risks stay at acceptable levels. These liability issues include safety, health, and environmental risks.

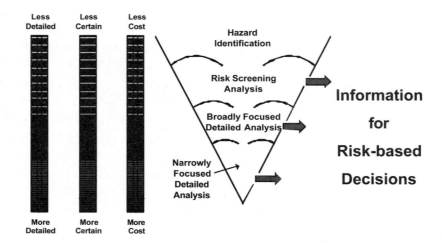

2.3 Levels of risk assessment

The goal of any risk assessment is to provide information that helps stakeholders make better decisions whenever the possibility of accidents exists. Therefore, the whole process of performing a risk assessment should focus on providing the type of risk information decision makers will need. The required types of information vary according to the following:

The types of issues being studied

The different stakeholders involved

The significance of the risks

The costs required to control the risks

The availability of information and data related to the issue being assessed

Information needs determine how the risk assessment should be performed.

The goal is to perform the least amount of risk assessment necessary to provide information that is *barely adequate* for decision making. In other words, do as little as possible to provide the information decision makers need. Although it is not always obvious in the beginning, decision makers can often make decisions using information that has very little detail or may be uncertain. In other cases, more complicated risk assessment information is necessary. The key is always to begin risk assessments at as general a level as possible and do more detailed studies only in areas where the additional risk assessment will help the decision maker. Unnecessary risk assessment doesn't benefit the decision maker. It also uses up time and money that could have been spent solving the problem or looking at other issues.

The figure on the previous page illustrates the idea of performing different levels of risk assessment. Each level can provide more detailed and better information, but the time, money, and energy required increases at each level. The filtering effect of each level allows only the most important issues to move into the next, more detailed, level of assessment. At any point, if enough information for decision making is gathered, then the risk assessment may end at that level. Not all levels of assessment will be performed for every issue that arises. In fact, most issues will probably be resolved through risk screening or broadly focused, detailed assessments.

At each level, the risk assessment may involve qualitative or quantitative risk characterizations. The following sections briefly describe each level of risk assessment.

Hazard identification. Hazards must be understood because they are the starting point for chains of events that lead to accidents. Although hazard identification doesn't usually provide information for decision making, it is an important step. Sometimes hazard identification is specifically performed using structured techniques. Other times, usually when the hazards of interest are well known, such structured techniques are not necessary. Overall, hazard identification focuses a risk assessment on hazards of interest and the types of accidents these hazards may create.

All risk assessments begin at this level. Analysts with little risk assessment experience and some training can successfully perform these types of risk assessments.

Risk screening assessment. In most situations, there are hundreds or even thousands of ways that accidents can occur. It is usually impractical to assess each of these possibilities in detail. Risk screening assessments are very general assessments that broadly describe risk and identify the most important areas for further investigation. Sometimes this level of assessment is enough to provide all of the information decision makers need; however, more detailed assessment of important issues is most common.

Once the hazards are understood, all risk assessments should begin at this level. Generally, analysts with fairly modest risk assessment experience and some training can successfully perform these types of assessments.

Broadly focused, detailed assessment. When specific activities or systems are found to have important or uncertain risks, broadly focused, detailed assessments are generally used. These assessments use structured tools for finding specific combinations of human errors, equipment failures, and external events that lead to consequences of interest. These assessments may also use qualitative or quantitative risk characterizations so that good risk management strategies can be defined.

Most risk assessments are broadly focused, detailed assessments that use qualitative risk characterizations or, at most, quantitative categorization. These risk assessments require analysts with training and experience. This is the most advanced level of assessment that someone without a specialty in risk assessment should try.

Narrowly focused, detailed analysis. When specific human errors, equipment failures, or external events are particularly important or uncertain, more narrowly focused, detailed risk assessments are needed. These assessments generally study specific issues in great detail, often involving many numeric calculations to describe the risk.

This level of assessment should be used only for those applications truly needing this level of information. Only analysts with special training and some supervised experience should try this level of risk assessment.

The following table lists the risk assessment methods discussed in this publication. The table indicates the levels of analysis for which each method is most often used.

Risk Assessment Method	Applicability to Various Levels of Risk Assessment			
	Hazard Identification	Risk Screening	Broadly Focused, Detailed Analysis	Narrowly Focused, Detailed Analysis
Pareto analysis		X		
Checklist analysis	X	X	X	X
Relative ranking/risk indexing		X	X	
Preliminary risk analysis (PrRA)		X		
Change analysis	X	X	X	X
What-if analysis	X	X	X	X
Failure modes and effects analysis (FMEA)			X	X
Hazard and operability (HAZOP) analysis			X	
Fault tree analysis (FTA)			X	X
Event tree analysis (ETA)		X	X	X
Event and causal factor charting				X
Preliminary hazard analysis (PrHA)	X	X		

Chapter 4
Principles of Risk Management

1.0 Risk Goals

It is hard to control risks without knowing where to aim or how closely you have come to hitting the target. Therefore, the first step in managing risk involves establishing risk management goals.

All operations in an organization present some risk. To determine whether operations are adequately controlled, management must establish some risk acceptance criteria. The criteria usually take the form of a frequency level, a consequence severity, or a combination of these two, with an understanding that the criteria should not be exceeded. A possible system failure that violates these criteria usually results in recommendations to better control the risks.

> ### Factors Affecting Risk Acceptance
>
> **Many factors influence our acceptance of risk:**
>
> - **Familiarity**
> - **Frequency**
> - **Control**
> - **Media attention**
> - **Consequence**
> - **Suddenness of consequence**
> - **Personal versus societal**
> - **Benefit**
> - **Dread**

2.0 Factors Affecting Risk Acceptance

In deciding how to manage risk, one key question is whether or not a risk is acceptable. Many factors affect our perception of acceptable risk. These include the following:

Familiarity — People are more comfortable and accepting of risk when they are personally familiar with the operation. For example, is a traveler more fearful of a bus accident or a plane crash? Which has the greater risk?

Frequency — Our belief in the frequency of an accident influences our risk acceptance. If we do not believe that the accident will happen, we are more likely to accept the risk.

Control — We accept more risk when we are personally in control, because we trust ourselves. For example, are you more afraid when you drive a car too fast or when you are the passenger in a speeding car?

Media attention — We fear problems that we are aware of and that we think are important and credible. Media coverage of issues increases our awareness of a problem and our belief in its credibility.

Consequence — We are not likely to accept risk for facilities that can have accidents with severe consequences. For example, an accident at a nuclear power plant could affect a large population. Therefore, we build very few such plants and we stringently regulate their safety. The risk related to coal-fired plants may be higher, but such plants are not as stringently regulated by the government.

Suddenness of consequence — The sooner we feel the impact of an event, the less likely we are to accept the risk. Would you risk your life to save your car from a carjacker? Would you risk your life by smoking cigarettes for 40 years?

Personal versus societal — We accept risk that affects only ourselves. We apply a higher standard to protect society.

Benefit — As the benefit we receive from an operation increases, we are more accepting of the risk. For example, driving a car is more risky than traveling by plane. Because of personal benefit, people are usually more accepting of driving than flying.

Dread — We have a strong fear or dread of risks whose severity we believe we cannot control. These risks are thought to be catastrophic, fatal, hard to prevent, inequitable, threatening to future generations, and involuntary. An example is the risk of cancer. People are fearful of anything that may cause cancer because of the nature of the disease, its treatment, and, in some cases, the low probability of recovery.

Issues of Acceptable Risk

- There is no practical definition
- Its perception varies among industries
- It is very hazard specific
- Even government agencies are not consistent
- There are contemporary comparisons that can be made

3.0 Issues of Acceptable Risk

With so many factors influencing our ideas about risk, it is nearly impossible for us to define "acceptable risk." Many companies and the government have tried, but everyone has a different understanding of "acceptable risk." For example, what risk is acceptable with the carcinogens benzene in gasoline and asbestos in public buildings? Even though defining acceptable risk is difficult, we should not give up on the idea. By setting a risk standard, organizations can more easily identify high-risk operations, can more appropriately allocate resources, and can measure the effectiveness of their risk reduction efforts.

The table on the next page is a summary of implied risk acceptance criteria from different government agencies for a variety of substances. Although the numbers listed are no longer valid, they show that acceptable risk is hard to determine.

Agency Interpretations of Significant Risk

Lifetime individual risks that agencies chose to regulate

Risk*	Substance (statute)
4×10^{-1}	Arsenic (OSHA)
2×10^{-1}	Ethylene dibromide (OSHA)
1×10^{-1}	Ethylene oxide (OSHA)
6×10^{-2}	Asbestos (OSHA)
3×10^{-2}	Arsenic from primary copper smelting (CAA)
2×10^{-2}	Coke oven emissions (CAA)
1×10^{-2}	Methylenedianiline (TSCA)
1×10^{-2}	Butadiene (TSCA)
1×10^{-2}	Uranium mines (CAA)
5×10^{-3}	Benzene from coke ovens (CAA)
2×10^{-3}	Benzene from fugitive emissions (CAA)
1×10^{-3}	Radionuclides from phosphate mines (CAA)
8×10^{-4}	Arsenic from glass manufacture (CAA)
8×10^{-4}	Radionuclides from DOE installations (CAA)
2×10^{-4}	Workers in coke ovens (OSHA)
1×10^{-4}	Radionuclides from NRC licensees (CAA)

*Probability of death given maximum regulated exposure

> **S — Spread out**
> **T — Transfer**
> **A — Accept**
> **A — Avoid**
> **R — Reduce**

4.0 Risk Management Categories

Risk can be managed in many different ways throughout the life cycle of the system. The following list describes the major categories of risk management strategies:

Spread out — Spread the loss exposure responsibility out among different entities, across operations, or across time

Transfer — Make others accept loss exposure responsibility

Accept — Live with the current loss exposure level or responsibility

Avoid — Cancel or delay the activity that involves the risk, or do not operate equipment that involves the risk

Reduce — Do something to reduce the accident potential

Category	Description	Example for a Possible Fishing Derby
S	Spread out	Ask local authorities to get involved in planning
T	Transfer	Make the applicants arrange safety patrols, emergency response
A	Accept	Do nothing
A	Avoid	Don't allow the derby
R	Reduce	Make the participants pass Coast Guard Auxiliary Boating Skills and Seamanship course

---

Accident Prevention Options

- ■ **Eliminate hazards**
- ■ **Prevent initiating events (incidents)**
- ■ **Add safeguards**
- ■ **Make safeguards more reliable**
- ■ **Reduce consequences**
- ■ **Reduce effects**

5.0 Accident Prevention Options

Accidents can be well controlled at any point in the chain of events producing the accident. The goal is to get the most for your money by doing the things that are most effective. The following sections describe each of the risk management options.

Eliminate hazards. Make processes inherently safer by eliminating hazards.

Examples:

- Eliminate energy sources:
    - pressure
    - heat
    - potential energy
    - kinetic energy, etc.
- Don't use hazardous materials and materials that can generate hazardous energy

Prevent initiating events (incidents). Reduce the likelihood of initiating events.

Examples:

- Eliminate error-likely situations that set people up for failure
- Perform inspections, tests, and preventive maintenance when needed
- Improve design ratings and factors of safety

Add safeguards. Provide multiple layers of safeguards, sometimes called layers of protection, in critical applications.

Examples:

- Add additional instrumentation, equipment, or safety interlocks, especially items with different design and operation
- Make the operators perform more surveillance and checks during operations

Make safeguards more reliable. Reduce the chance of safeguard failures.

Examples:

- Eliminate error-likely situations that set people up for failure
- Perform additional or more frequent inspections, tests, and preventive maintenance
- Improve design ratings and factors of safety
- Make sure that enough people are assigned to operations and maintenance departments

Reduce consequences. Make processes inherently safer by reducing the severity of consequences.

Examples:

- Reduce energy stored or generated as:
  - pressure
  - heat
  - potential energy
  - kinetic energy, etc.
- Keep only small inventories of hazardous materials and materials that can generate hazardous energy
- Use other, less hazardous, materials in place of more hazardous materials
- Provide shutdown and response systems to limit consequences. These include alarms and quick-shutoff valves.

Reduce effects. Protect people and other valuables from consequences.

Examples:

- Provide emergency response training
- Provide personal protective equipment
- Move people away from the danger zones
- Train the employees and community to find shelter in a safe place

Guidelines for choosing risk management options

We can measure how well our actions are working, or will work, to reduce risk. Three general measures of risk management success are shown in the table below.

An effective risk management activity must strike a good balance among the three criteria in the above table.

Chapter 5
Principles of Risk
Communication

1.0 Definition of Risk Communication

Communicating about risk is an important and challenging part of doing business with corporations, the government, and the military. In fact, some professional communicators believe that, in modern society, all communication is risk communication. The National Research Council's definition shows what risk communication is and what it is not.

> *The Interactive process of exchanging information and opinion among individuals, groups, and institutions involving multiple messages about the nature of risk...*

What risk communication *is*:

An interactive process. This process (1) requires an understanding of factors that affect the communication process and ways in which people think about risk and risk information, and (2) provides for ongoing response and discussion with key audiences and affected parties.

An exchange of information and opinion. The goals of this information exchange include (1) improving people's understanding and (2) changing impressions, attitudes, and behaviors.

A process that involves individuals, groups, and institutions. These participants see your communication as (1) objective (a product of research, statistics, and technical expertise) or (2) subjective (based on personal values and experience).

A process that concerns the nature of risk. The nature of risk is more than simply the frequency and consequence of an event. It involves questions such as, "What can happen to me, personally?" and "What can I do to keep from having to deal with this?" It also involves the history of the risk and the future associated with addressing it.

Risk communication is *not:*

A set of gimmicks or techniques to avoid debate or criticism

A collection of unclear messages

An afterthought during the final stages of risk assessment

A promise of general agreement or consensus about risk management actions

Risk-based Decision-making Process

2.0 Risk Communication in the Risk-based Decision-making Process

Skilled risk communication must take place throughout the risk-based decision-making process. The graphic above shows that communicating about risk is a part of all phases of the process. Risk-based decisions will rarely produce the desired results if the decisions are made without considering the opinion of those who will be affected; that is, the stakeholders.

The involvement of all stakeholders in the risk-based decision-making process is essential. Every effort should be taken to include appropriate representatives from both internal and external organizations, as well as individuals affected by key risk-based decisions. Involving other stakeholders enhances the risk-based decision-making process in the following ways:

• It creates a sense of "buy-in" with the final decision among the stakeholders

• It allows stakeholders to understand other points of view

• It facilitates the consideration of ideas that would have been overlooked without stakeholder involvement

A balance of stakeholder involvement is required, though. Involving too many stakeholders in all aspects of the risk-based decision-making process can be overwhelming to the stakeholders and counterproductive to the decision-making objectives. At the same time, bringing in stakeholders after the decision-making process has progressed too far can also be counterproductive. These issues must be considered early in the decision-making process.

When dealing with members of the public, remember that concerned citizens feel they have fought for and won the right to have a say in environmental, health, and safety matters that may affect their lives. The standard for "successful" risk communication in this setting has risen steadily. Citizens have come to expect notification, an exchange of views, and, whenever possible, consensus on key issues. They want to weigh the benefits against the potential downsides of economic and environmental decisions. They do not want surprises.

3.0 Risk Communication Cycle

Risk communication activities usually follow six basic steps. Any or all may take place at any time throughout the risk-based decision-making process, and not all activities are necessary for each situation. The step you choose to take and when you choose to take it depend on the circumstances. Audiences or groups of stakeholders may choose to be involved at different levels and at different times in the process. However, all stakeholders must be genuinely given the opportunity to participate. Their opinions and concerns must be addressed, even if common ground cannot be found.

Assess

Identify audiences. These can include mariners, industry, environmental groups, and citizen action groups, as well as local, state, and federal government

Determine how well the community understands the risks

Evaluate existing communication efforts

- Evaluate available communication media

Prepare and train

Become familiar with basic principles and techniques of risk communication

Learn and practice basic presentation skills

Broaden outreach and dialogue

Encourage community and stakeholder involvement

Set up ways to exchange ideas with the community

Improve community outreach efforts

Plan and coordinate

Set up a communication plan and timeline

Establish a mission statement and set measurable goals

Identify the primary concerns of each audience

Select paths of communication for each audience

Identify communication tools for each audience

Communicate risk

Develop and test messages

Create communication materials

Arrange events to exchange ideas

Start up dialogue with key audiences

Follow up and evaluate

Risk communication is a two-way street and an ongoing process. You must, therefore, do the following:

Follow up and respond to stakeholder input, questions, and concerns

Evaluate whether the communication process is effective

> **Successful Risk Communication**
>
> - Factors influencing personal values
> - Three principles of risk communication
> - Seven cardinal rules of risk communication

4.0 Successful Risk Communication

Risk communication is the exchange of information, opinions, and ideas between you and the stakeholders. It is much more than communicating information and expecting stakeholders to come around to your side of the table. While you are presenting information from your point of view, so are many others. When faced with opposing views, participants in risk communication often become confused and may ignore input from one or all sides of an issue. This causes communication efforts to fail. Successful risk communication requires all stakeholders to know that their input has been heard and considered.

Successful risk communication also happens when all parties involved believe they are receiving quality information, and each person considers the values of the various participants. It is a mistake to assume that hazards, consequences, and remedies are viewed the same way by everyone.

Factors influencing personal values

These factors may include the following:

- Cultural background
- Shared interests, concerns, and fears
- Social attitudes
- Ability to understand technical language
- A personal stake in the process or outcome

4.1 Three principles of risk communication

Understanding the values of your stakeholders and how their values influence opinions and beliefs is only one factor in a successful risk communication program. Research into risk communication offers other guidelines that affect your communication efforts. These principles fall into three general categories:

Perception = Reality

Even if the stakeholder's perception is not based on fact, it cannot be dismissed. In risk communication, you must deal with expected or known perceptions that may disagree with your technical understanding. These perceptions are still real to the person who holds them and must be respected as that individual's reality.

Goal = Trust + Credibility

The goal of successful risk communication is reached through the development of a basic trust with the stakeholders, often influenced by past experience, and the soundness of the information communicated. Low-trust, high-risk situations require more care in developing the risk messages.

Communication = Skill

Even when trust is earned, results are positive, and leaders are sincere, the success of risk communication depends on the communication skills of those involved. Factors that affect how risk messages are understood include the following:

Sincerity of the source (YOU)

Content of the message (WHAT you say)

Delivery of the message (HOW you say it)

Planning (WHERE you say it)

4.2 Seven cardinal rules of risk communication

Even if you establish a trusting relationship with your stakeholders, risk communication can provide a tangled web of information. Though this may be the information age, *more* information is not always *better* information. Information coming from many sources may contain opposing messages. Therefore, it is up to you to make sure that the messages you communicate are clear, accurate, and understood (if not accepted). You must also provide ways to accept the same kind of messages from your stakeholders. While the three principles of risk communication will guide you through the beginning of your risk communication efforts, the following seven cardinal rules of risk communication will help you carry out an effective program.

1. Accept and involve the public (actually, all of the stakeholders) as a partner. Paying lip service to the risk communication process is worse than having no risk communication at all.

2. Plan carefully and evaluate your efforts. If you do not know where you are going, how will you know when you get there? Set measurable goals in the beginning.

3. Listen to your audience. Act on and respond to their concerns.

4. Be honest and open. The human qualities of the person who represents you have a more lasting impact than the words of the message. You become the message.

5. Plan and work with other reliable sources. Involve reliable third parties — clergy, local elected officials, emergency responders, employees — in the risk communication process.

6. Meet the needs of the media. Most members of the public receive their information from the media.

7. Speak clearly and with understanding. Even a well-structured and well-delivered message can be lost if it is delivered by an unskilled speaker.

The following table provides a few factors affecting the ways in which risk is understood, along with situations that tend to increase and decrease public concern.

Factors Affecting Risk Perception		
Factor	Conditions Associated with *Increased* Public Concern	Conditions Associated with *Decreased* Public Concern
Disastrous potential	Deaths and injuries at the same time in the same place	Random deaths and injuries
Familiarity	Unfamiliar	Familiar
Understanding	Mechanisms or process not understood	Mechanisms or process understood
Controllability (own)	Uncontrollable	Controllable
Exposure willingness	Involuntary	Voluntary
Effects on children	Children specifically at risk	Children not specifically at risk
Effects timing	Delayed effects	Immediate effects
Future generation effects	Risk to future generations	No risk to future generations
Victim identification	Identifiable victims	Statistical victims
Dread	Effects dreaded	Effects not dreaded
Trust in institutions	Lack of trust in responsible institutions	Trust in responsible institutions
Media attention	Much media attention	Little media attention
Accident history	Major or minor accidents	No major or minor accidents
Equity	Uneven spread of risks and benefits	Even spread of risk and benefits
Benefits	Unclear benefits	Clear benefits
Reversibility	Effects irreversible	Effects reversible
Origin	Caused by human actions or failures	Caused by acts of nature of God

---

Developing Key Messages

- **Premise statement**
- **Support points**
- **Enhancements**

5.0 Developing Key Messages

Keeping these risk communication principles and rules in focus throughout the risk communication process helps you work toward your goal, in which all parties involved believe they have received quality information. Nowhere in the process are these principles and rules more important than in developing your key messages. Your key messages — no more than three, each of which is no more than 15 to 20 words — are the heart of the communication process. Begin by considering what is most important in the minds of your audiences. Environment? Health of their children? Job security? Knowing what kinds of information your audience wants will help you prepare messages more effectively.

Messages generally have three parts:

Premise statement. The fundamental message. The one thing you want your audiences to know or understand about you and what you do.

Support points. Develop two to four key support points for your premise statement. Use easy-to-understand facts or figures, stories or comparisons, historical data, or quotes from reliable third-party sources.

Enhancements. These are examples or sketches of your story in action, elements that give your story a human face — a person who developed a new safety process, for instance, or an end-user who benefits personally from the fact that the Coast Guard is here.

The next page provides a checklist to help you develop and present better risk communication messages.

Risk Message Checklist*

	Information about the Nature of Risks
	What are the hazards of concern?
	What is the probability of exposure to each hazard?
	What is the spread of exposure (who is exposed to the hazard)?
	How likely is it that someone will be harmed from a given exposure to each hazard?
	What are the sensitivities of different populations to each hazard?
	How do exposures interact with exposures to other hazards?
	What are the qualities of the hazard?
	What is the total population risk?
	Information about the Nature of Benefits
	What are the benefits associated with the hazard?
	What is the probability that the expected benefit will actually follow the activity?
	What are the qualities of the benefits?
	Who benefits and in what ways?
	How many people benefit and how long do benefits last?
	Which groups get an unequal share of the benefits?
	What is the total benefit?
	Information on Options
	What are the options regarding the hazards in question?
	What is the effectiveness of each option?
	What are the risks and benefits of other actions and of not acting?
	What are the costs and benefits of each option and how are they spread out?
	Uncertainties in Knowledge about Risks
	What are the weaknesses of available data?
	What are the assumptions on which estimates are based?
	How sensitive are the estimates to changes in the assumptions?
	How sensitive is the decision to changes in the estimates?
	What other reviews have been made; what differences exist and why?
	Information on Management
	Who is responsible for the decision?
	What issues have legal importance?
	What constrains the decision?

*Improving Risk Communication, National Research Council

6.0 Dealing with an Angry Public

Risk communication often takes place among parties who are on opposite sides of an issue. One or all of the parties, particularly *the public*, may be angry.

Why is the public angry?

Members of the public may be angry for any of several reasons:

Because they have been negatively affected by something

Because they are fearful of being negatively affected by something

Because they disagree in principle with something that is happening

Traditional responses to an angry public have included (1) proving that the public has not been negatively affected by something, (2) attempting to put aside public fears, and (3) downplaying differences in values. In addition, many organizations find well-known supporters for their point of view.

Develop a mutual gains approach to dealing with an angry public

The traditional approach does not work, because a public that prefers not to take any additional risk does not trust the supporters. In addition, advocacy groups sometimes take advantage of conflict for their own ends. Often, the media increase distrust, and the public does not understand that the differing interests are valid. The mutual gains approach to dealing with an angry public is more effective when you do the following:

Accept concerns of the other side

Encourage joint fact finding

Offer commitments to reduce impacts if they do occur; promise to make up for unintended effects

Accept responsibility, admit mistakes, and share power

Act in a trustworthy way at all times

Focus on building long-term relationships

The mutual gains approach to dealing with an angry public has, at its core, effective risk communication. During this process, you must do the following:

- **Take the initiative** — do not wait until you are on the defensive

- **Seek agreement** — do not try to convince people they are wrong; give them a reason to do what you want them to do

- **Emphasize outcomes** — do not lose sight of your long-term objectives

- **Maintain credibility** — do not say anything that you know is not true; do not make promises you cannot keep

- **Enhance legitimacy** — act as you want others to act

> ## Working with the Media
>
> **Three keys to success with the media:**
> - use conflict creatively
> - put substance in a sound bite
> - present the story visually

7.0 Working with the Media

Many stakeholders affected by your issues, whether angry or not, get most of their information from the media. The media are essentially the pipeline through which information to the public must ultimately pass. Therefore, the media are vital to the success of any risk communication program. Knowing how the media work and understanding their role in the communication process can help you communicate with this important audience and, thus, with the audiences the media reach for you.

Journalists work under tight deadlines and management constraints. They often have little technical expertise or understanding, and they cover viewpoints, not truths. Your story, whether good or bad, competes for air time or print space with many others. Remember, bad news sells, and that is what journalists are first to cover. While you cannot prevent media coverage of the bad news, you can work effectively to see that all information is fairly and accurately presented. The Coast Guard has developed several formal protocols for working with the media. Work with the appropriate Coast Guard public affairs office when you know the decision-making process will require contact with the media.

Three keys to success with the media

1. **Use conflict creatively.** Every media interview is an opportunity to show your organization's commitment to its mission. It is a chance to spread your message and improve public opinion.

2. **Put substance in a sound bite.** Most television stories are 45 to 90 seconds long; you have about 20 seconds to get your point across. Focus on your key messages, and always answer questions honestly. Do not give in to the temptation to tell the reporter more than he or she, or the audience, wants to know.

3. **Present the story visually.** Provide easy-to-understand charts, graphs, and photographs for print media, and video or audiotapes for the electronic media.

Some Interview "Dos" and "Don'ts"

■**Do**
- ◆ speak to the physical audience
- ◆ consider the editorial process
- ◆ refer to key messages often
- ◆ state important facts first
- ◆ say you don't know if you don't
- ◆ be responsive, but maintain control
- ◆ keep answers short
- ◆ keep it simple
- ◆ assume the camera is always on
- ◆ be serious

■**Don't**
- ◆ say "No comment"
- ◆ speculate or guess
- ◆ lie
- ◆ speak off the record

Some Interview "Dos" and "Don'ts"

The following are some important "dos" and "don'ts" to remember when talking with the media. While these suggestions are not magical formulas for success, they should help you avoid some of the most common media interview pitfalls.

Do

Speak to the physical audience. Speak to the reporter or camera crew. If addressing a gathering of people, speak to that audience.

Consider the editorial process. The reporter is looking for a 10- to 20-second sound bite containing your actions and concerns.

Refer to your key messages often. Do this at every opportunity.

State the most important facts first. Who, what, when, where, why, and how. Speak directly and simply.

Say you don't know if you don't. Do not try to snow the questioner. The questioner will have greater respect for you and your operations if you do not waste time trying to dance around the issue. Say "I don't know, but as soon as I can get that information, I'll get back to you." Then do it.

Be responsive, but maintain control. Do not lose your cool with a questioner who seems pushy or technically uninformed.

Keep your answers short. They are more easily understood and less likely to be edited by the media.

Keep it simple. Do not be technical. Remember, you are talking to people who do not share your knowledge of your organization. Do not use jargon or acronyms.

Assume that TV cameras and microphones are always on. Assume they are recording your words, actions, and expressions.

Be serious. Any attempt at humor will fail with some listeners, and may embarrass you as well.

Don't

Say "No comment." The questioner will think you are trying to hide something. If you cannot discuss something because it involves matters of a confidential nature or because you do not know, say so.

Speculate or guess. Do not allow yourself to be drawn into answering hypothetical questions or into debates with third parties who are not present.

Lie. Be honest and factual.

Speak off the record. With the media, there is no such thing. Assume that anything you say in an interview — or before or after an interview — is fair game for publication or broadcast.

Chapter 6
Risk Assessment Tools

1.0 Commonly Used Risk Assessment Tools

There are many hazard and risk assessment tools. The pages that follow provide a brief overview of 12 commonly used tools. They include the following:

1. Pareto analysis
2. Checklist analysis
3. Relative ranking/risk indexing
4. Preliminary risk analysis (PrRA)
5. Change analysis
6. What-if analysis
7. Failure modes and effects analysis (FMEA)
8. Hazard and operability (HAZOP) analysis
9. Fault tree analysis (FTA)
10. Event tree analysis (ETA)
11. Event and causal factor charting
12. Preliminary hazard analysis (PrHA)

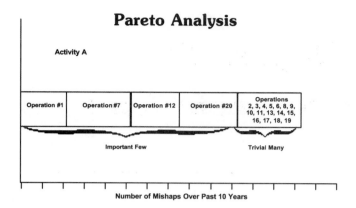

2.0 Summary of Pareto Analysis

Pareto analysis is a prioritization technique that identifies the most significant items among many. This technique employs the *80-20* rule, which states that about 80 percent of the problems or effects are produced by about 20 percent of the causes.

Brief summary of characteristics

- Used as a risk assessment technique at any level, from activity level to system level

- Yields broad, quantitative results that are graphically depicted on simple bar charts

- Depending on the information analyzed, generally requires some form of data tracking

- Applicable to any activity or operating system

Most common uses

- Most often used to rank activity or system accidents

- Can be used to rank the causes that contribute to accidents

- Also used to evaluate the risk improvement that results from activity or system modifications with "before" and "after" data

Variability in levels of risk assessment resolution. Deciding how to group elements of an activity or system for a Pareto analysis is an inherently subjective exercise. It produces significant variability in (1) the time required to perform the analysis and (2) the level of resolution in the results. Grouping elements at too high a level may mask significant variations among elements in each group. On the other hand, grouping elements at too low a level may falsely indicate relative importances of individual components.

Dependent on availability and applicability of data. The quality of Pareto analyses is completely dependent on the availability of relevant and reliable data for the activity or system being analyzed. A diligent focus on collecting meaningful data is critical to a successful Pareto analysis.

2.1 Limitations of Pareto Analysis

Although Pareto analysis is highly effective in identifying the most significant contributors to activity or system problems, this technique has three limitations:

Focuses only on the past. Pareto analysis develops risk-related characteristics for an activity or system based solely on the numbers and types of problems encountered in the past. While Pareto analysis offers a valuable look at key contributors to past problems, the exclusive reliance on historical data can be misleading in the following ways:

(1) The data underrepresent events that, luckily, have not happened yet or have occurred rarely but that, statistically, are just as likely as events that have occurred more frequently. This can skew decisions and resource allocations, especially when a relatively small total number of problems has occurred for individual components or types of components.

(2) Recent changes in operating practices, maintenance plans, equipment configurations, etc., may invalidate historical trends, or at least reduce their accuracy. This situation can also skew decisions and resource allocations, both when relatively recent changes have not been in place long enough to affect the data or when data are analyzed over extremely long time intervals during which numerous changes have been made.

2.2 Procedure for Pareto Analysis

The procedure for performing a Pareto analysis consists of the following eight steps.

1. **Define the activity or system of interest.** Specify and clearly define the boundaries of the activity or system for which risk-related information is needed.

2. **Define the specific risk-related factors of merit.** Specify the metrics that best characterize the problems of interest. These factors can be the number of accidents, failures, near misses, etc. Virtually any metric can serve as the basis for a Pareto analysis.

3. **Subdivide the activity or system for analysis.** Section the activity or system into its major elements, such as operations or subsystems. The analysis will begin at this level.

4. **Determine which elements of the activity or system lead to the problems of interest.** Not every element of an activity or system neces-

sarily contributes to every type of problem that the activity or system can experience. If specific accidents are of interest, omit some elements of an activity or system from the analysis.

5. **Collect and organize relevant risk data for elements of the activity or system.** Use data to estimate the contributions of activity or system elements that were not screened from consideration in the previous step.

6. **Plot the data on Pareto charts.** Present the data graphically on bar-line charts, showing the contributions of each activity or system element to the problems of interest.

7. **Further subdivide the elements of the activity or system (if necessary or otherwise useful).** If data are not available at the current level of analysis, further subdivide selected elements of the activity or system to successively finer levels of resolution until applicable data are found. Even when data are available at higher levels of the hierarchy, further subdivision helps identify and emphasize the key contributors to risk-related characteristics. Generally, the goal is to minimize the level of resolution necessary for an analysis.

8. **Use the results in decision making.** Use the estimated risk-related factors of merit to help make key decisions.

Checklist Analysis

Evaluation Points	Yes	No	Not Evaluated	Comments
Subject Area 1				
Evaluation Point 1-1	✓			
Evaluation Point 1-2	✓			
Evaluation Point 1-3		✓		Recommendation A
•				
•				
•				
Subject Area 2				
Evaluation Point 2-1			✓	
Evaluation Point 2-2	✓			
Evaluation Point 2-3	✓			
•				
•				
Subject Area 3				
•				
•				
•				

3.0 Summary of Checklist Analysis

Checklist analysis is a systematic evaluation against preestablished criteria in the form of one or more checklists.

Brief summary of characteristics

- A systematic approach built on the historical knowledge included in checklist questions

- Used for high-level or detailed analysis, including root cause analysis

- Applicable to any activity or system, including equipment issues and human factors issues

- Generally performed by an individual trained to understand the checklist questions. Sometimes performed by a small group, not necessarily risk analysis experts

- Based mostly on interviews, documentation reviews, and field inspections

- Generates qualitative lists of conformance and nonconformance determinations, with recommendations for correcting nonconformances

- The quality of evaluation is determined primarily by the experience of people creating the checklists and the training of the checklist users

Most common uses

- Used most often to guide teams through inspections of systems

- Also used as a supplement to or integral part of another method, especially what-if analysis, to address specific requirements

- A special, graphical type of checklist called a Root Cause Map™ is particularly effective for root cause analysis.

3.1 Limitations of Checklist Analysis

Although checklist analysis is highly effective in identifying various system hazards, this technique has two key limitations:

Likely to miss some potential problems. The structure of checklist analysis relies exclusively on the knowledge built into the checklists to identify potential problems. If the checklist does not address a key issue, the analysis is likely to overlook potentially important weaknesses.

Traditionally only provides qualitative information. Most checklist reviews produce only qualitative results, with no quantitative estimates of risk-related characteristics. This simplistic approach offers great value for minimal investment, but it can answer more complicated risk-related questions only if some degree of quantification is added, possibly with a relative ranking/risk indexing approach.

3.2 Procedure for Checklist Analysis

The procedure for performing a checklist analysis consists of the following steps.

1. **Define the activity or system of interest.** Specify and clearly define the boundaries for which risk-related information is needed.

2. **Define the problems of interest for the analysis.** Specify the problems of interest that the analysis will address. These may include safety problems, environmental issues, economic impacts, etc.

3. **Subdivide the activity or system for analysis.** Section the subject into its major elements. These may include locations, tasks, or subsystems. The analysis will begin at this level.

4. **Gather or create relevant checklists for the problems of interest.** Identify and collect lists of important questions or issues related to the type of potential problems within the scope of the analysis. If useful checklists are not available, consider developing your own checklists with the assistance of subject matter experts.

5. **Respond to the checklist questions.** Use a team of subject matter experts to respond to each of the checklist questions. Develop recommendations for improvement wherever the risk of potential problems seems uncomfortable or unnecessary.

6. **Further subdivide the elements of the activity or system (if necessary or otherwise useful).** Further subdivision of selected elements may be necessary if more detailed analysis of one or more elements is desired. Section those elements into successively finer levels of resolution until further subdivision will (1) provide no more valuable information or (2) exceed the the organization's control or influence to make improvements. Generally, the goal is to minimize the level of resolution necessary for an analysis.

7.0 **Use the results in decision making.** Evaluate the recommendations from the analysis and implement those that will bring more benefits than costs over the life cycle of the activity or system.

3.3 Example: Offsite Environmental Protection Checklist

Question	Yes	No	Comments
I. CHEMICAL HAZARD AWARENESS			
1. Are there any chemicals handled that are particularly sensitive from an environmental standpoint (carcinogens, volatile toxics, pesticides, odorants)? List them.			
2. Do you know the effects each chemical will have (following a catastrophic release):			
— directly on employee health?			
— directly on public health?			
— directly to vegetation?			
— directly to animal life?			
— indirectly to human life (such as by transmitting of persistent toxics through vegetation or animals)?			
— indirectly to all life (such as by non-lethal contamination of water and air)?			
3. Has the company performed consequence modeling (toxic dispersion, fire effects, blast effects, etc.) of worst-case events related to each of these chemicals?			
II. EFFLUENT STREAMS			
1. Have all effluent streams been identified and characterized?			
2. Do emission points include:			
— stacks, relief, and vents?			
— ventilation exhausts?			
— surface water runoff?			
— discharges to city sewers?			
— discharges to surface water bodies?			
— discharges or seepage to groundwater?			

Offsite Environmental Protection Checklist Example (Continued)

3. Are any of them hazardous or potentially hazardous? List them.			
4. Are scrubbers required on any stream? List them.			
5. Are the consequences catastrophic if they fail?			
6. Could any hazardous materials from spills or releases reach the waste treatment plant?			
7. Are there any hazards of sewered materials during normal and abnormal operation, considering:			
— runaway reactions?			
— flammable concentrations, either from the sewered material or from reactions (e.g., hydrogen evolution) in the sewer?			
— toxic fumes?			
— environmental contamination?			
— cross-contamination of process and sanitary sewers?			
8. Are effluents monitored (e.g., sampled) for unacceptable emissions? How?			
9. Could a catastrophic release occur in the time between measurement and alarm or notification?			
III. SURFACE RUNOFF			
1. Does surface water runoff require any special treatment?			
2. Is surface drainage adequate?			
3. Can it be protected (e.g., with sandbags) from process material spills?			
IV. OPERATIONS			
1. Are special precautions necessary to meet environmental requirements and protect human health? List them.			
2. Are there specific environmental restrictions that will limit operations? List them.			
3. Will maintenance work require special precautions to prevent odor problems, air pollution, or sewer contamination? List them.			

Offsite Environmental Protection Checklist Example (Continued)

4. Releases from process:			
— Could releases from the process area travel off site?			
— Would any hazards result from these releases? List them.			
— Are any special precautions necessary for leak-prone equipment (e.g., bellows, rotating seals)? List them.			
5. Have offsite effects been considered in the selection of discharge locations for:			
— vents?			
— reliefs?			
— flares?			
— scrubbers?			
V. CONTAINMENT			
1. What prevents or limits spills during operations?			
— Is there remote shutdown/isolation capability?			
— Are manual isolation valves useable and properly located?			
— Is use of these isolation valves periodically tested?			
— Are there excess flow valves, check valves, or automatic shutdowns?			
— Are railcars and trucks protected against collision or inadvertent movement during loading/unloading?			
— Are hoses inspected/pressure tested/ replaced regularly?			
— Are there high level and/or pressure alarms on storage tanks (particularly remote tanks)?			
2. Are storage areas diked?			
3. Are the dikes large enough?			
4. Are any dikes damaged or breached?			
5. Are programs implemented to ensure the integrity of the dikes?			
6. If the dike overflowed (e.g., because of the fire			

Offsite Environmental Protection Checklist Example (Continued)

fighting activities), would an offsite release of interest occur?			
7. Can hazardous materials be rapidly and safely transferred to a safe storage vessel, in an emergency situation? Is such a capability necessary?			
8. Is there periodic training in isolation and containment procedures?			
VI. AREA DETECTION			
1. Are there toxic/flammable gas monitors and alarms in process and material storage areas?			
2. Do procedures specify how often they are tested? Are these followed?			
3. Do procedures specify how to test/calibrate detectors? Are these followed?			
4. Is there a need for additional detection methods/devices such as:			
— routine operator/maintenance rounds			
— point sensors?			
— closed-circuit television?			
— other types of detection?			
VII. EMERGENCY RESPONSE TO RELEASES			
1. Are containment and clean-up techniques defined for all materials?			
2. Is the technique usable in the work area/offsite?			
3. Are there written procedures for handling small releases?			
4. Are operators, maintenance workers, or contractors expected to contain and clean up releases?			
5. Have the people who will clean up releases been trained?			
6. Are appropriate protective equipment and clean-up supplies on hand in readily accessible locations?			
7. Are different procedures or supplies required to handle products of undesired reactions?			
8. Are there any suppression, absorption, or cleaning			

Offsite Environmental Protection Checklist Example (Continued)

media that are prohibited (because they are not effective, they react with some other chemical present in the area, or they are harmful to equipment)? List them.			
9. Are any media of this type available in the area?			
10. If water is prohibited, are there warning signs in the area?			
11. Are workers trained when to call the spill response team?			
12. Is the spill response team capable of handling all releases?			
— Are there enough spill response team members available during the day shift? off-shifts?			
— Do emergency personnel have defined procedures to follow when entering a unit?			
— Is enough proper protective equipment available to the emergency personnel? Are enough SCBAs available?			
— Will protective gear withstand exposure to process chemicals?			
— Is release suppression, collection, and cleanup equipment available in the facility? from mutual aid groups? from the community? List the resources.			
13. Is there a defined procedure for calling outside emergency response teams?			
14. Is there a defined procedure for notifying corporate management and public authorities?			
15. Is there a defined procedure for evacuating the unit, facility, or community?			
16. Is there an emergency command center, and how is it staffed?			
17. Have these procedures been practiced in the last year?			
18. Are there adequate, reliable means of reporting emergencies to a response team and to applicable government officials or agencies?			

Offsite Environmental Protection Checklist Example (Continued)

VIII. EVACUATION PLANS			
1. Are there adequate, reliable means of sounding an evacuation alarm to all building or area occupants?			
2. Is there a written evacuation plan for the unit, facility, and community?			
3. If the process operations cannot be shut down, can they be left on automatic control?			
4. Are assembly points, evacuation routes, and alternates clearly marked?			
5. Are emergency control centers established?			
6. Are there re-entry and cleanup procedures?			
7. Has the plan been coordinated with local authorities?			
8. Has the plan been tested and appropriately revised?			
9. Are up-to-date emergency shutdown and evacuation plans posted?			
10. Are they effectively communicated to transient workers (e.g., outside contractors)?			
IX. OFFSITE CONSEQUENCES			
1. Have the nearest and/or largest onsite and offsite populations been identified? List them.			
2. Have the distances to these populations been measured? List them.			
3. Are there any locations that present special evacuation problems (e.g., schools, hospitals, nursing homes, large population centers)? List them.			
4. Are there any sensitive environments (endangered species, wetlands, etc.) that could be affected by a release, fire, or explosion? List them.			

4.0 Summary of Relative Ranking/Risk Indexing

$$\text{Ranking Index} = \text{Fn}\left(\text{Factor}_1, \text{Factor}_2, \ldots\right)$$

Some example ranking index factors:
- vessel owner
- flag state
- class society
- vessel inspection and boarding history
- vessel type
- etc.

The relative ranking/risk indexing technique assesses the attributes of a vessel, shore facility, or operation to calculate index numbers. These index numbers are useful for making relative comparisons of various alternatives and can, in some cases, be correlated to actual performance estimates. This method scores facilities or operations in a number of categories, called factors, to generate the index values. Of course, the factors and scoring process are very different for various applications.

Brief summary of characteristics

A systematic process built on the experience of the ranking system developers

Generally performed by a small group who are not necessarily risk experts but who have been trained to understand the ranking system. Sometimes performed by an individual.

Based mostly on interviews, documentation reviews, and field inspections

Used most often as a top-level risk assessment technique

Applicable to almost any facility

A technique that generates:

- index numbers that provide ordered lists of priorities

- lists of attributes that are the dominant contributors to problems

A technique in which the quality of evaluation is determined primarily by the relevance and quality of the ranking tool that is used and the training of the users

Most common uses

- Can be used to compare various options for facility modifications

4.1 Limitations of the Relative Ranking/Risk Indexing Technique

The relative ranking/risk indexing technique can provide a high-level assessment of the risks associated with a range of activities; however, the following are a number of limitations that should be considered before selecting this method:

Results can be difficult to tie to absolute risks. The relative ranking/risk indexing technique uses various indexing tools to derive risk scores for particular activities; however, these scores are used only for relative comparisons of one activity to another. The scores do not provide information about the absolute risk associated with activities.

Appropriate ranking tool may not exist. Each relative ranking/risk indexing tool provides a structured methodology for (1) collecting risk-related data, (2) performing specific, often arithmetic, calculations on it, and (3) assessing the resulting index scores derived from the calculations. The tools are typically well documented to allow personnel who are not experts in risk assessment to use them effectively. However, the tools are typically focused on a particular type of risk to be evaluated; if an applicable tool does not exist, resources must be invested to develop one. For simple applications on one unit, custom development of a tool may be relatively inexpensive, possibly a day or two of development time. For broader, standardized applications, considerably more development and validation time may be needed.

Does not account for unique situations. Relative ranking/risk indexing tools are specifically designed to focus on a particular type of risk. They are typically well-documented and very structured to allow personnel who are not expert in risk assessment to effectively use the tools. However, the rigid structure and necessity to comply with the structure of a tool makes it difficult to account for situations outside the scope of the particular tool. This may make it necessary to develop a new tool.

4.2 Procedure for Relative Ranking/Risk Indexing

Define the scope of the study. Clearly define the activity that will be analyzed and the desired decisions or outcomes expected from the study.

Select the ranking tool that will be used. The tools used to conduct a relative ranking review vary widely in form and complexity. The analyst can select from among existing tools or may choose to develop one specifically suited for a particular type of application.

Collect scoring information. Each ranking tool will use different types of information about vessels, facilities, or operations to calculate index values. This information must be reliably collected by the analysis team.

Calculate ranking indexes. Following the instructions for the tool selected, the analyst calculates risk index numbers and summarizes the results to facilitate comparisons among reviewed areas.

Use the results in decision making. The results for the study may be used alone or in conjunction with other factors, such as cost. The results may identify the most important contributors to the index numbers and will help the analyst determine if corrective actions or design modifications should be undertaken to reduce the anticipated risk.

Preliminary Risk Analysis

| | | | Frequency | | | | | | Recommen- |
No.	Accident	Most Significant Contributors	1	2	3	RIN	Certainty	Safeguards	dations
1.1	Acute hazard exposure: workers	Dropped objects	3	4	3	1.815	Medium	Personnel qualifications	Consider establishing fatigue guidelines
		Physical injuries during handling operations							
		Slips, trips, or falls during handling operations						Promulgation and enforcement of industry standards: personal protective equipment and safe work practices	

(table title: Preliminary Risk Analysis)

5.0 Summary of Preliminary Risk Analysis

Preliminary risk analysis is a streamlined accident-centered risk assessment approach. The primary objective of the technique is to characterize the risk associated with significant accident scenarios. This team-based approach relies on systematic examination of the issues by subject matter experts and stakeholders. The team postulates combinations of accidents, most significant contributors to accidents, and safeguards. The analysis also characterizes the risk of the accidents and identifies recommendations for reducing risk. The graphic above shows a portion of a worksheet from a preliminary risk analysis.

Brief summary of characteristics

- Systematic approach based on the HAZOP analysis technique

- Analyzes accidents that may occur during normal operations

- Performed using a team of subject matter experts

- An analysis technique that generates

  - qualitative descriptions of potential problems

  - quantitative estimates of risk

  - lists of recommendations for reducing risk

  - quantitative evaluations of recommendation effectiveness

Most common uses

- Used primarily for generating risk profiles across a broad range of activities

5.1 Preliminary Risk Analysis Terminology

Definitions

The following terms are commonly used in preliminary risk analysis:

Activity. A collection of tasks or a single task performed in support of an objective

Screening. Determining at a high level that an item is of low risk and will not need to be analyzed in detail

Accident. A mishap or loss

Most significant contributor. A scenario or initiating event (cause) that, if not prevented or mitigated, may result in an accident

Safeguard. Engineered systems (hardware) or administrative controls for (1) reducing the frequency of occurrence of significant contributors or (2) reducing the likelihood or the severity of accidents

Frequency. A score indicating the expected number of occurrences per year of the relevant accident category

Risk index number (RIN). A relative measure of the overall risk associated with an accident

Certainty. The confidence in the frequency assessments provided by the analysis team

Recommendations. Suggestions for (1) reducing the risk associated with an accident or (2) providing more extensive evaluation of specific issues

Risk matrix. A matrix depicting the risk profile of issues analyzed. Each cell in the matrix indicates the number of accidents having that frequency and consequence.

Frequency range. A lower and upper limit representing the estimated frequency of occurrence of an accident category

5.2 Limitations of Preliminary Risk Analysis

Although preliminary risk analysis is effective and efficient for identifying high-risk accidents, this tool has two primary limitations:

- **High-level analysis.** The preliminary risk analysis focuses on potential accidents of an activity; therefore, the failures leading to accidents are not explored in much detail. The high-level, general nature of the analysis introduces a level of uncertainty in the results.

- **General recommendations.** One result of the analysis is the development of recommendations for reducing risk. Due to the high-level nature of the analysis, these recommendations are typically general in nature instead of focused on attacking specific issues.

5.3 Procedure for Preliminary Risk Analysis

The procedure for performing a preliminary risk analysis consists of the following five steps.

1. **Determine the scope of the preliminary risk analysis.** Determining the scope includes identifying the hazards and activities that will be analyzed.

2. **Screen low-risk activities.** Screening low-risk items streamlines the analysis by eliminating in-depth review of these items.

3. **Analyze accidents.** Evaluating possible accidents, and screening them when appropriate, is the fundamental activity in the preliminary risk analysis. This involves identifying accidents. It also involves identifying the most significant contributors and safeguards, and characterizing the risk associated with the accidents. Recommendations for reducing risk or reducing uncertainty are also developed.

4. **Generate a risk profile.** The risk information generated from the preliminary risk analysis can be sorted and reported in a variety of ways to aid in decision making.

5. **Evaluate the benefit of risk reduction recommendations.** Before a recommendation is implemented, the benefit or risk reduction realized from implementing the recommendation should be calculated and considered.

Change Analysis

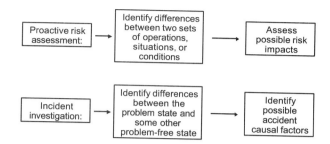

6.0 Summary of Change Analysis

Change analysis looks systematically for possible risk impacts and appropriate risk management strategies in situations where change is occurring. This includes situations in which system configurations are altered, operating practices or policies are changed, new or different activities will be performed, etc.

Brief summary of characteristics

Systematically explores all of the differences from normal operations and conditions that may introduce significant risks or may have contributed to an actual accident

Is used effectively for proactive hazard and risk assessment in changing situations and environments as well as during accident investigations

Can be used to identify changes in overall risk profiles, when used in conjunction with other methodologies such as the preliminary risk analysis methodology.

Is a conceptually simple tool that can be implemented in a reasonable amount of time

Most common uses

Generally applicable to any situation in which change from normal configuration, operations, or activities is likely to significantly affect risks.

Can be used as an effective root cause analysis method as well as a predictive risk assessment method

6.1 Limitations of Change Analysis

Highly dependent on points of comparison. Change analysis relies on comparisons of two systems or activities to identify weaknesses in one of the systems in relation to the other. Thus, an appropriate point of comparison is very important.

Does not inherently quantify risks. Change analysis does not traditionally involve quantification of risk levels; however, the results of change analysis can be used with other risk assessment methods that produce quantitative risk characterizations, such as the preliminary risk analysis method.

Strongly dependent on the expertise of those participating in the analysis. The knowledge and experience of the people participating in a change analysis strongly affect their ability to recognize and evaluate notable differences between the system or activity of interest and the point of comparison. In addition, the expertise and experience of the participants certainly affect the quality of the risk management options that are identified.

6.2 Procedure for Change Analysis

The procedure for performing a change analysis consists of the following six steps:

1. **Define the system or activity of interest.** Specify and clearly define the boundaries of any physical system or operational activity of interest.

2. **Establish the key differences from some point of comparison.** Choose a comparable physical system or operational activity that is well understood and would expose weaknesses in the system or activity of interest when comparisons are made. Then, systematically identify all of the differences, regardless of how subtle, between the system or activity of interest and the chosen point of comparison.

3. **Evaluate the possible effects of notable differences.** Examine each of the identified differences, and decide whether each has the potential to contribute to losses of interest. This evaluation often generates recommendations to better control any significant risks associated with notable differences.

4. **Characterize the risk impacts of notable differences (if necessary).** Use some type of risk characterization approach, such as the quantitative risk categorization method used with the preliminary risk analysis methodology, to indicate how the differences affect the risks of various types of losses. (This type of risk categorization is seldom necessary when change analysis is used during an accident investigation).

5. **Examine important issues in more detail (if necessary).** Analyze important potential accidents further with other risk analysis tools or other accident investigation tools.

6. **Use the results in decision making.** Use the results of the analysis to identify significant system or activity vulnerabilities and to make effective recommendations for managing the risks.

What-if Analysis

Questions	Responses
■ "What if {a specific accident} occurs?" ■ "What if {a specific system} fails?" ■ "What if {a specific human error} occurs?" ■ "What if {a specific external event} occurs?"	"{Immediate system vessel condition} "potentially leading to {accident of interest} "if {applicable safeguards} fail"

7.0 Summary of What-if Analysis

What-if analysis is a brainstorming approach that uses broad, loosely structured questioning to (1) postulate potential upsets that may result in accidents or system performance problems and (2) ensure that appropriate safeguards against those problems are in place.

Brief summary of characteristics

- A systematic, but loosely structured, assessment relying on a team of experts brainstorming to generate a comprehensive review and to ensure that appropriate safeguards are in place

- Typically performed by one or more teams with diverse backgrounds and experience that participate in group review meetings of documentation and field inspections

- Applicable to any activity or system

- Used as a high-level or detailed risk assessment technique

- Generates qualitative descriptions of potential problems, in the form of questions and responses, as well as lists of recommendations for preventing problems

- The quality of the evaluation depends on the quality of the documentation, the training of the review team leader, and the experience of the review teams

Most common uses

- Generally applicable for almost every type of risk assessment application, especially those dominated by relatively simple failure scenarios

- Occasionally used alone, but most often used to supplement other, more structured techniques (especially checklist analysis)

7.1 Limitations of What-if Analysis

Although what-if analysis is highly *effective* in identifying various system hazards, this technique has three limitations:

Likely to miss some potential problems. The loose structure of what-if analysis relies exclusively on the knowledge of the participants to identify potential problems. If the team fails to ask important questions, the analysis is likely to overlook potentially important weaknesses.

Difficult to audit for thoroughness. Reviewing a what-if analysis to detect oversights is difficult because there is no formal structure against which to audit. Reviews tend to become *"mini-what-ifs,"* trying to stumble upon oversights by the original team.

Traditionally provides only qualitative information. Most what-if reviews produce only qualitative results; they give no quantitative estimates of risk-related characteristics. This simplistic approach offers great value for minimal investment, but it can answer more complicated risk-related questions only if some degree of quantification is added.

7.2 Procedure for What-if Analysis

The procedure for performing a what-if analysis consists of the following seven steps:

1. **Define the activity or system of interest.** Specify and clearly define the boundaries for which risk-related information is needed.

2. **Define the problems of interest for the analysis.** Specify the problems of interest that the analysis will address (safety problems, environmental issues, economic impacts, etc.).

3. **Subdivide the activity or system for analysis.** Section the subject into its major elements (e.g., locations on the waterway, tasks, or subsystems). The analysis will begin at this level.

4. **Generate what-if questions for each element of the activity or system.** Use a team to postulate hypothetical situations (generally beginning with the phrase "what if ...") that team members believe could result in a problem of interest.

5. **Respond to the what-if questions.** Use a team of subject matter experts to respond to each of the what-if questions. Develop recommendations for improvements wherever the risk of potential problems seems uncomfortable or unnecessary.

6. **Further subdivide the elements of the activity or system (if necessary or otherwise useful).** Further subdivision of selected elements of the activity or system may be necessary if more detailed analysis is desired. Section those elements into successively finer levels of resolution until fur-

ther subdivision will (1) provide no more valuable information or (2) exceed the organization's control or influence to make improvements. Generally, the goal is to minimize the level of resolution necessary for a risk assessment.

7. **Use the results in decision making.** Evaluate recommendations from the analysis and implement those that will bring more benefits than they will cost in the life cycle of the activity or system.

Failure Modes and Effects Analysis

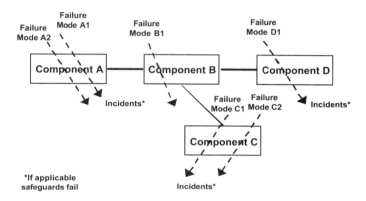

8.0 Summary of Failure Modes and Effects Analysis (FMEA)

FMEA is a qualitative reasoning approach best suited for reviews of mechanical and electrical hardware systems. The FMEA technique (1) considers how the failure modes of each system component can result in system performance problems and (2) ensures that appropriate safeguards against such problems are in place. A quantitative version of FMEA is known as failure modes, effects, and criticality analysis (FMECA).

Brief summary of characteristics

- A systematic, highly structured assessment relying on evaluation of component failure modes and team experience to generate a comprehensive review and ensure that appropriate safeguards against system performance problems are in place

- Used as a system-level and component-level risk assessment technique

- Applicable to any well-defined system

- Sometimes performed by an individual working with system experts through interviews and field inspections, but also can be performed by an interdisciplinary team with diverse backgrounds and experience participating in group review meetings of system documentation and field inspections

- A technique that generates qualitative descriptions of potential performance problems (failure modes, causes, effects, and safeguards) as well as lists of recommendations for reducing risks

- A technique that can provide quantitative failure frequency or consequence estimates

Most common uses

- Used primarily for reviews of mechanical and electrical systems, such as fire suppression systems.

- Used frequently as the basis for defining and optimizing planned equipment maintenance because the method systematically focuses directly and individually on equipment failure modes

- Effective for collecting the information needed to troubleshoot system problems

8.1 Limitations of FMEA

Although the FMEA methodology is highly effective in analyzing various system failure modes, this technique has four limitations:

Examination of human error is limited. A traditional FMEA uses potential equipment failures as the basis for the analysis. All of the questions focus on how equipment functional failures can occur. A typical FMEA addresses potential human errors only to the extent that human errors produce equipment failures of interest. Misoperations that do not cause equipment failures are often overlooked in an FMEA.

Focus is on single-event initiators of problems. A traditional FMEA tries to predict the potential effects of specific equipment failures. These equipment failures are generally analyzed one by one, which means that important combinations of equipment failures may be overlooked.

Examination of external influences is limited. A typical FMEA addresses potential external influences (environmental conditions, system contamination, external impacts, etc.) only to the extent that these events produce equipment failures of interest. External influences that directly affect facility and worker safety are often overlooked in an FMEA if they do not cause equipment failures.

Results are dependent on the mode of operation. The effects of certain equipment failure modes often vary widely, depending on the mode of system operation. A single FMEA generally accounts for possible effects of equipment failures only during one mode of operation or a few closely related modes of operation. More than one FMEA may, therefore, be necessary for a system that has multiple modes of operation.

8.2 Procedure for FMEA

The procedure for performing an FMEA consists of the following nine steps.

1. **Define the system of interest.** Specify and clearly define the boundaries of the system for which risk-related information is needed.

2. **Define the accidents of interest for the analysis.** Specify the problems of interest that the analysis will address. These may include safety issues or failures in systems.

3. **Choose the type of FMEA approach for the study.** Select a hardware approach (bottom-up), functional approach (top-down), or hybrid approach for applying FMEA.

4. **Subdivide the system for analysis.** Section the system according to the type of FMEA approach selected.

5. **Identify potential failure modes for elements of the system.** Define the fundamental ways that each element of the system can fail to achieve its intended functions. Determine which failures can lead to accidents of interest for the analysis.

6. **Evaluate potential failure modes capable of producing accidents of interest.** For each potential failure that can lead to accidents of interest, evaluate the following:

   • The range of possible effects

   • Ways in which the failure mode can occur

   • Ways in which the failure mode can be detected and isolated

   • Safeguards that are in place to protect against accidents resulting from the failure mode

7. **Perform quantitative evaluation (if necessary).** Extend the analysis of potentially important failures by characterizing their likelihood, their severity, and the resulting levels of risk. FMEAs that incorporate this step are referred to as failure modes, effects, and criticality analyses (FMECAs).

8. **Transition the analysis to another level of resolution (if necessary or otherwise useful).** For top-down FMEAs, follow-on analyses at lower (i.e., more detailed) levels of analysis may be useful for finding more specific contributors to system problems. For bottom-up FMEAs, follow-on analyses at higher (i.e., less detailed) levels of analysis may be useful for characterizing performance problems in broader categories. Typically, this would involve system and subsystem characterizations based on previous component-level analyses.

9. **Use the results in decision making.** Evaluate recommendations from the analysis and implement those that will bring more benefits than they will cost over the life cycle of the system.

Hazard and Operability Analysis

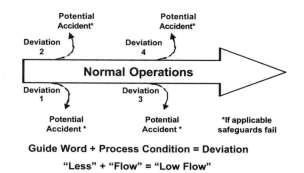

Guide Word + Process Condition = Deviation

"Less" + "Flow" = "Low Flow"

9.0 Summary of Hazard and Operability (HAZOP) Analysis

The HAZOP analysis technique uses a systematic process to (1) identify possible deviations from normal operations and (2) ensure that appropriate safeguards are in place to help prevent accidents. The HAZOP technique uses special adjectives (such as "more," "less," "no," etc.) combined with process conditions (such as speed, flow, pressure, etc.) to systematically consider all credible deviations from normal conditions. The adjectives, called guide words, are a unique feature of HAZOP analysis.

Brief summary of characteristics

- A systematic, highly structured assessment relying on HAZOP guide words and team brainstorming to generate a comprehensive review and ensure that appropriate safeguards against accidents are in place

- Typically performed by a multidisciplinary team

- Applicable to any system or procedure

- Used most as a system-level risk assessment technique

- Generates primarily qualitative results, although some basic quantification is possible

Most common uses

- Used primarily for identifying safety hazards and operability problems of continuous process systems

- Also used to review procedures and sequential operations

9.1 Limitations of the HAZOP Technique

Requires a well-defined system or activity. The HAZOP process is a rigorous analysis tool that systematically analyzes each part of a system or activity. To apply the HAZOP guide words effectively and to address the potential accidents that can result from the guide word deviations, the analysis team must have access to detailed design and operational information. The process systematically identifies specific engineered safeguards (e.g., instrumentation, alarms, and interlocks) that are defined on detailed engineering drawings.

Time consuming. The HAZOP process systematically reviews credible deviations, identifies potential accidents that can result from the deviations, investigates engineering and administrative controls to protect against the deviations, and generates recommendations for system improvements. This detailed analysis process requires a substantial commitment of time from both the analysis facilitator and other subject matter experts, such as workers, engineering personnel, equipment vendors, etc.

Focuses on one-event causes of deviations. The HAZOP process focuses on identifying single failures that can result in accidents of interest. If the objective of the analysis is to identify all combinations of events that can lead to accidents of interest, more detailed techniques should be used. One example would be fault tree analysis.

9.2 Procedure for HAZOP Analysis

The procedure for performing a HAZOP analysis consists of the following five steps:

1. **Define the system or activity.** Specify and clearly define the boundaries of the system or activity for which hazard and operability information is needed.

2. **Define the problems of interest for the analysis.** Specify the problems of interest that the analysis will address. These may include health and safety issues, environmental concerns, etc.

3. **Subdivide the system or activity and develop deviations.** Subdivide the system or activity into sections that will be individually analyzed. Then apply the HAZOP guide words that are appropriate for the specific type of equipment in each section.

4. **Conduct HAZOP reviews.** Systematically evaluate each deviation for each section of the system or activity. Document recommendations and other information collected during the team meetings, and assign responsibility for resolving team recommendations.

5. **Use the results in decision making.** Evaluate the recommendations from the analysis and the benefits they are intended to achieve. The benefits may include improved safety and environmental performance or cost savings. Determine implementation criteria and plans.

Fault Tree Analysis

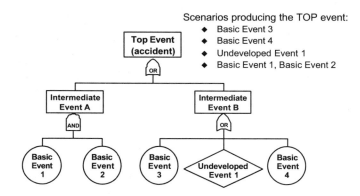

Scenarios producing the TOP event:
- Basic Event 3
- Basic Event 4
- Undeveloped Event 1
- Basic Event 1, Basic Event 2

10.0 Summary of Fault Tree Analysis

Fault tree analysis (FTA) is an analysis technique that visually models how logical relationships between equipment failures, human errors, and external events can combine to cause specific accidents. The fault tree presented in the figure above illustrates how combinations of equipment failures and human errors can lead to a specific type of accident.

Below is a summary of the graphics most commonly used to construct a fault tree.

Top event and intermediate events

The rectangle is used to represent the TOP event and any intermediate fault events in a fault tree. The TOP event is the accident that is being analyzed. Intermediate events are system states or occurrences that somehow contribute to the accident.

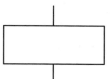

Basic events

The circle is used to represent basic events in a fault tree. It is the lowest level of resolution in the fault tree.

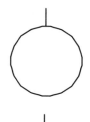

Undeveloped events

The diamond is used to represent human errors and events that are not further developed in the fault tree.

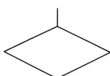

AND gates

The event in the rectangle is the output event of the AND gate below the rectangle. The output event associated with this gate exists only if all of the input events exist simultaneously.

OR gates

The event in the rectangle is the output event of the OR gate below the rectangle. The output event associated with this gate exists if at least one of the input events exists.

Inhibit gates

The event in the rectangle is the output event of the INHIBIT gate below the rectangle. This gate is a special case of the AND gate. The output event associated with this gate exists only if the input event exists and if the qualifying condition (the inhibiting condition shown in the oval) is satisfied.

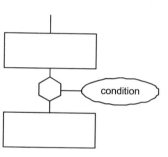

Transfer symbols

Transfer symbols are used to indicate that the fault tree continues on a different page.

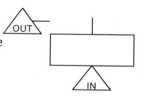

Brief summary of characteristics

- Models the possible combinations of equipment failures, human errors, and external conditions that can lead to a specific type of accident

  Used most often as a system-level risk assessment technique

  Includes human errors and common-cause failures

  Performed primarily by an individual working with system experts through interviews and field inspections

  A risk assessment technique that generates

  - qualitative descriptions of potential problems and combinations of events causing specific problems of interest

  - quantitative estimates of failure frequencies and likelihoods, and relative importances of various failure sequences and contributing events

  - lists of recommendations for reducing risks

  - quantitative evaluations of recommendation effectiveness

Most common uses

- Generally applicable for almost every type of risk assessment application, but used most effectively to address the fundamental causes of specific accidents dominated by relatively complex combinations of events

- Can be used as an effective root cause analysis tool in several applications

  - to understand the causal factors of an accident

  - to determine the actual root causes of an accident

10.1 Limitations of Fault Tree Analysis

Although fault tree analysis is highly effective in determining how combinations of events and failures can cause specific system failures, this technique has three notable limitations:

Narrow focus. Fault tree analysis examines only one specific accident of interest. To analyze other types of accidents, other fault trees must be developed.

Art as well as science. The level of detail, types of events included in a fault tree analysis, and organization of the tree vary significantly from analyst to analyst. Assuming two analysts have the same technical knowledge, there will still be notable differences in the fault trees that each would generate for the same situation. However, given the same scope of analysis and limiting assumptions, different analysts should produce comparable, if not identical, results.

Quantification requires significant expertise. Using fault tree analysis results to make statistical predictions about future system performance is complex. Only highly skilled analysts can reliably perform such quantifications.

In addition, analysts often become so focused on equipment and systems that they forget to address human and organizational issues adequately in their models. While this is not an inherent limitation of fault tree analysis, it is worth noting.

10.2 Procedure for Fault Tree Analysis

The procedure for performing a fault tree analysis consists of the following eight steps:

1. **Define the system of interest.** Specify and clearly define the boundaries and initial conditions of the system for which failure information is needed.

2. **Define the TOP event for the analysis.** Specify the problem of interest that the analysis will address. This may be a specific quality problem, shutdown, safety issue, etc.

3. **Define the treetop structure.** Determine the events and conditions (i.e., intermediate events) that most directly lead to the TOP event.

4. **Explore each branch in successive levels of detail.** Determine the events and conditions that most directly lead to each intermediate event. Repeat the process at each successive level of the tree until the fault tree model is *complete*.

5. **Solve the fault tree for the combinations of events contributing to the TOP event.** Examine the fault tree model to identify all the possible combinations of events and conditions that can cause the TOP event of interest. A combination of events and conditions sufficient and necessary to cause the TOP event is called a *minimal cut set*.

6. **Identify important dependent failure potentials and adjust the model appropriately.** Study the fault tree model and the list of minimal cut sets to identify potentially important dependencies among events. Dependencies are single occurrences that may cause multiple events or conditions to occur at the same time. This step is qualitative common cause failure analysis.

7. **Perform quantitative analysis (if necessary).** Use statistical characterizations regarding the failure and repair of specific events and conditions in the fault tree model to predict future performance for the system.

8. **Use the results in decision making.** Use results of the analysis to identify the most significant vulnerabilities in the system and to make effective recommendations for reducing the risks associated with those vulnerabilities.

Event Tree Analysis

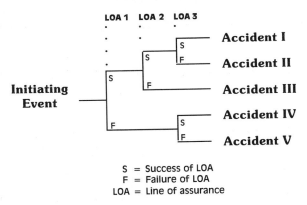

S = Success of LOA
F = Failure of LOA
LOA = Line of assurance

11.0 Summary of Event Tree Analysis

Event tree analysis (ETA) is a technique that logically develops visual models of the possible outcomes of an initiating event. As illustrated above, event tree analysis uses decision trees to create the models. The models explore how safeguards and external influences, called lines of assurance, affect the path of accident chains.

Event tree terminology

The following terms are commonly used in an event tree analysis:

Initiating event. The occurrence of some failure with the potential to produce an undesired consequence. An initiating event is sometimes called an incident.

Line of assurance (LOA). A protective system or human action that may respond to the initiating event

Branch point. Graphical illustration of (usually) two potential outcomes when a line of assurance is challenged; physical phenomena, such as ignition, may also be represented as branch points

Accident sequence or scenario. One specific pathway through the event tree from the initiating event to an undesired consequence

Brief summary of characteristics

- Models the range of possible accidents resulting from an initiating event or category of initiating events

- A risk assessment technique that effectively accounts for timing, dependence, and domino effects among various accident contributors that are cumbersome to model in fault trees

- Performed primarily by an individual working with subject matter experts through interviews and field inspections

- An analysis technique that generates the following:

    - qualitative descriptions of potential problems as combinations of events producing various types of problems (range of outcomes) from initiating events

    - quantitative estimates of event frequencies or likelihoods and relative importances of various failure sequences and contributing events

    - lists of recommendations for reducing risks

    - quantitative evaluations of recommendation effectiveness

Most common uses

Generally applicable for almost any type of risk assessment application, but used most effectively to model accidents where multiple safeguards are in place as protective features

11.1 Limitations of Event Tree Analysis

Although event tree analysis is highly effective in determining how various initiating events can result in accidents of interest, this technique has two limitations.

Limited to one initiating event. An event tree is not an exhaustive approach for identifying various causes that can result in an accident. Other analysis techniques, such as HAZOP, what-if, checklist, or FMEA, should be considered if the objective of the analysis is to identify the causes of potential accidents.

Can overlook subtle system dependencies. The paths at each branch point in an event tree are conditioned on the events that occurred at previous branch points along the path. For example, if ignition of a flammable release does not occur, there is no fire for subsequent lines of assurance (e.g., fire protection systems) to fight. In this way, many dependencies among lines of assurance are addressed. However, lines of assurance can have subtle dependencies, such as common components, utility systems, operators, etc. These subtle dependencies can be easily overlooked in event tree analysis, leading to overly optimistic estimates of risk.

11.2 Procedure for Event Tree Analysis

The procedure for performing an event tree analysis consists of the following seven steps:

1. **Define the system or activity of interest.** Specify and clearly define the boundaries of the system or activity for which event tree analyses will be performed.

2. **Identify the initiating events of interest.** Conduct a screening-level risk assessment to identify the events of interest or categories of events that the analysis will address. Categories include such things as groundings, collisions, fires, explosions, and toxic releases.

3. **Identify lines of assurance and physical phenomena.** Identify the various safeguards (lines of assurance) that will help mitigate the consequences of the initiating event. These lines of assurance include both engineered systems and human actions. Also, identify physical phenomena, such as ignition or meteorological conditions, that will affect the outcome of the initiating event.

4. **Define accident scenarios.** For each initiating event, define the various accident scenarios that can occur.

5. **Analyze accident sequence outcomes.** For each outcome of the event tree, determine the appropriate frequency and consequence that characterize the specific outcome.

6. **Summarize results.** Event tree analysis can generate numerous accident sequences that must be evaluated in the overall analysis. Summarizing the results in a separate table or chart will help organize the data for evaluation.

7. **Use the results in decision making.** Evaluate the recommendations from the analysis and the benefits they are intended to achieve. Benefits can include improved safety and environmental performance, cost savings, or additional output. Determine implementation criteria and plans. The results of the event tree may also provide the basis for decisions about whether to perform additional analysis on a selected subset of accident scenarios.

Event and Causal Factor Charting

CF = Causal Factor
* = Item of Note

12.0 Summary of Event and Causal Factor Charting

Event and causal factor charting is a written or graphical description for the time sequence of contributing events associated with an accident. The charts produced in event charting consist of the following elements:

Condition. A distinct state that facilitates the occurrence of an event. A condition may be equipment status, weather, employee health, or anything that affects an event.

Event. A point in time defined by a specific action occurring

Accident. Any action, state, or condition in which a system is not meeting one or more of its design intents. Includes actual accidents and near misses. This event is the focus of the analysis.

Primary event line. The key sequence of occurrences that led to the accident. The primary event line provides the basic nature of the event in a logical progression, but it does not provide all of the contributing causes. This line always contains the accident, but it does not necessarily end with an accident event. The primary event line can contain both events and conditions.

Primary events and conditions. The events and conditions that make up the primary event line

Secondary event lines. The sequences of occurrences that lead to primary events or primary conditions. The secondary event lines expand the development of the primary event line to show all of the contributing causes for an accident. Causal factors are almost always found in secondary event lines, and most event and causal factor charts have more than one secondary event line. Note that the secondary event lines can contain both events and conditions.

Secondary events and conditions. The events and conditions that make up a secondary event line

Causal factors. Key events or conditions that, if eliminated, would have prevented an accident or reduced its effects. Causal factors are such things as human error or equipment failure, and they commonly include the following:

- The initiating event for an accident
- Each failed safeguard
- Each reasonable safeguard that was not provided

Items of note. Undesirable events or conditions identified during an analysis that must be addressed or corrected but did not contribute to the accident of interest. These are shown as separate boxes outside the event chain.

12.1 Limitations of Event and Causal Factor Charting

Although event charting is an effective tool for understanding the sequence of contributing events that lead to an accident, it does have two primary limitations:

Will not necessarily yield root causes. Event charting is effective for identifying causal factors. However, it does not necessarily ensure that the root causes have been identified, unless the causal factor is the root cause.

Overkill for simple problems. Using event charting can overwork simple problems. A two-event accident probably does not require an extensive investigation of secondary events and conditions.

12.2 Procedure for Event and Causal Factor Charting

The procedure for event and causal factor charting consists of the following five steps:

1. **Gather and organize data.** Collect known data for actors associated with the accident. An actor is a person, parameter, or object that has an action in the event chain. Organize the data into a timeline. Review data for consistency and gaps. This step is not always necessary for simple events.

2. **Select the accident.** Define the accident of interest. If there is more than one accident, choose the last one to occur.

3. **Define the primary sequence of events leading to the accident.** Outline the *thumbnail sketch* of the sequence of events leading to the accident. Work backward from the accident, making certain that each subsequent event is the one that most directly leads to the previous event.

- Draw events as rectangles

    - describe events specifically with one noun and one action verb
    - use quantitative descriptions when possible to characterize events
    - include the timing of the event when known
    - use solid lines for known events and dashed lines for assumed events

- Draw conditions as ovals

    - describe conditions specifically using a form of the verb *to be*
    - use quantitative descriptions to characterize conditions
    - include the timing and duration of the condition when known
    - use solid lines for known conditions and dashed lines for assumed conditions

	Action	Condition
Fact	▭	⬭
Supposition	⬚	⬭
Verb (Past Tense)	Active: walked, called, turned on, etc.	Passive: was, were

4. **Complete the model by adding secondary events and conditions.** Add secondary events and conditions as appropriate to ensure that all events and conditions leading to an accident are sufficient and necessary to cause the accident. Add events as appropriate to display the contributors to the secondary events and conditions.

5. **Identify causal factors and items of note.** Designate the underlying contributors to the accident as causal factors. Document any items of note.

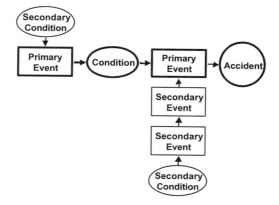

Preliminary Hazard Analysis

Example PrHA Worksheet

Area: ——————————————— Meeting Date: ———————————————
Drawing Number: —————————— Team Members: ——————————

Hazard: Potential Accident	Cause	Major Effects	Accident Severity Category	Corrective/Preventive Measures Suggested

13. Summary of Preliminary Hazard Analysis

The preliminary hazard analysis (PrHA) technique is a broad, initial study used in the early stages of system design. It focuses on (1) identifying apparent hazards, (2) assessing the severity of potential accidents that could occur involving the hazards, and (3) identifying safeguards for reducing the risks associated with the hazards. This technique focuses on identifying weaknesses early in the life of a system, thus saving time and money that might be required for major redesign if the hazards were discovered at a later date.

Brief summary of characteristics

- Relies on brainstorming and expert judgment to assess the significance of hazards and assign a ranking to each situation. This helps in prioritizing recommendations for reducing risks.

- Typically performed by one or two people who are knowledgeable about the type of activity in question. They participate in review meetings of documentation and field inspections, if applicable.

- Applicable to any activity or system

- Used as a high-level analysis early in the life of a process

- Generates qualitative descriptions of the hazards related to a process. Provides a qualitative ranking of the hazardous situations; this ranking can be used to prioritize recommendations for reducing or eliminating hazards in subsequent phases of the life cycle.

- Quality of the evaluation depends on the quality and availability of documentation, the training of the review team leader with respect to the various analysis techniques employed, and the experience of the review teams

Most common uses

- Generally applicable for almost any type of risk assessment application, but focuses predominantly on identifying and classifying hazards rather than evaluating them in detail

- Most often conducted early in the development of an activity or system, when there is little detailed information or there are few operating procedures. Often a precursor to further risk assessment.

13.1 Limitations of Preliminary Hazard Analysis

Because the preliminary hazard analysis technique is typically conducted early in the process, before other analysis techniques are practical, this methodology has two primary limitations:

Generally requires additional follow-up analyses. Because the PrHA is conducted early in the process and uses preliminary design information, additional analyses are generally required to more fully understand and evaluate hazards and potential accidents identified by the PrHA team.

Quality of the results is highly dependent on the knowledge of the team. At the time of a PrHA, there are few or no fully developed system specifications and little or no detailed design information. Therefore, the risk assessment relies heavily on the knowledge of subject matter experts. If these experts do not participate in the risk assessment, or if the system is a new technology having little or no early operational history, the results of the PrHA will reflect the uncertainty of the team in many of its assessments and assumptions.

13.2 Procedure for Preliminary Hazard Analysis

The procedure for conducting a preliminary hazard analysis consists of the following steps.

1. **Define the activity or system of interest.** Specify and clearly define the boundaries of the activity or system for which preliminary hazard information is needed.

2. **Define the accident categories of interest and the accident severity categories.** Specify the problems of interest that the risk assessment will address (e.g., health and safety concerns, environmental issues). Specify the accident severity categories that will be used to prioritize resources for risk reduction efforts.

3. **Conduct review.** Identify the major hazards and associated accidents that could result in undesirable consequences. Also, identify design criteria or alternatives that could eliminate or reduce the hazards.

4. **Use the results in decision making.** Evaluate the risk assessment recommendations and the benefits they are intended to achieve (e.g., improved safety and environmental performance, cost savings). Determine implementation criteria and plans.

Overview of Influence Diagraming

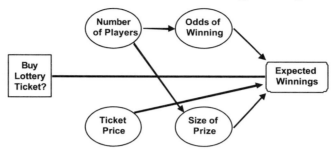

14.0 Overview of Influence Diagraming

An influence diagram is a powerful tool for identifying hazards, evaluating risk, determining risk management options, and communicating hazards. By providing a framework for the decision, influence diagrams link the real world with the analytical model. An example influence diagram is shown in the figure above.

As can be seen, influence diagrams are constructed of three elements: branches, directed arcs, and nodes. Nodes are used to capture the various stages for the problem. There are three types of nodes:

- Decision nodes (e.g., buy lottery ticket?)

- Event nodes (e.g., odds of winning)

- Value nodes representing the results of a decision process (e.g., expected winnings)

The nodes are drawn as squares, ovals, and rounded rectangles, respectively. They are typically arranged from left to right, to match the flow of time.

Branches can be used in two ways. They can show possible outcomes of random events, and they can describe possible alternatives. Branches are drawn as line segments between nodes.

Directed arcs are used to show possible conditional dependence. They are drawn as arrows connecting nodes, with the direction indicating dependence. In the example above, they are used to show the effects of the various quantities (e.g., number of players) on later quantities (e.g., odds of winning).

Though this overview is qualitative, influence diagrams can be used quantitatively by applying probabilities to model future events based on the influence of previous events.

Overview of Commonly Used Risk Analysis Tools

Hazard Risk Analysis Methods	Summary of Method	More Common Uses
Pareto Analysis	Pareto analysis is a ranking technique based only on past data that identifies the most important items among many. This technique uses the 80-20 rule, which states that about 80 percent of the problems are produced by about 20 percent of the causes.	• Can be used for any type of system, process, or activity as long as enough historical data are available • Usually used to find the most important risk contributors so that more detailed risk assessments can be performed later
Checklist Analysis	Checklist analysis is an evaluation against existing guidelines in the form of one or more checklists.	• Useful for any type of system, process, or activity, especially when suitable checklists of accident prevention requirements or best practices exist • Most often used when the use of other, more precise, methods such as FMEA and HAZOP analysis are not possible or practical • Checklist analysis is frequently combined with what-if analysis to add depth and allow for creative thinking • An error-likely situation checklist is a special type of checklist for use in human reliability analysis • A walkthrough analysis is a type of human factors checklist helpful for understanding equipment characteristics as they relate to worker actions • The Root Cause Map is a special graphical checklist used in incident investigations to determine root causes
Relative Ranking/Risk Indexing	Relative ranking/risk indexing uses measurable features of a vessel, shore facility, port, or waterway to calculate index numbers that are useful for comparing risks of different options. These index numbers can, in some cases, be related to actual performance estimates.	• Suited to any type of analysis, especially when only relative priorities are needed, as long as a proper scoring tool exists
Preliminary Risk Analysis (PrRA)	PrRA is a simplified approach to accident-based risk assessment. The main goal of the technique is to define the risk related to important accident scenarios. This team-based approach relies on subject matter experts examining the issues. The team suggests possible accidents, most important contributors to accidents, and protective features. The analysis also identifies the risk of the accidents and identifies recommendations for reducing risk.	• Used for producing risk profiles across a range of activities. • Coarse risk analysis is a special type of PrRA and is deviation-based instead of accident-based
Change Analysis	Change analysis looks logically for possible risk effects and proper risk management strategies in changing situations (e.g., when system layouts are changed, when operating practices or policies change, when new or different activities will be performed).	• Used for any situation in which change from normal setup, operations, or activities is likely to affect risks. • Can be used as an effective root cause analysis method, as well as a forecasting risk assessment method

Overview of Commonly Used Risk Analysis Tools (continued)

Hazard Risk Analysis Methods	Summary of Method	More Common Uses
What-if Analysis	What-if analysis is a problem-solving approach that uses loosely structured questioning to (1) suggest upsets that may result in accidents or system performance problems and (2) make sure the proper safeguards against those problems are in place.	• Useful for any type of system, process, or activity • Most often used when the use of other, more precise, methods (e.g., FMEA and HAZOP analysis) are not possible or practical • What-if analysis is frequently combined with checklist analysis to add structure to the analysis
Failure Modes and Effects Analysis (FMEA)	FMEA is a reasoning approach best suited to reviews of mechanical and electrical hardware systems. The FMEA technique (1) considers how the failure modes of each system component can result in system performance problems and (2) makes sure the proper safeguards are in place. A quantitative version of FMEA is known as failure modes, effects, and criticality analysis (FMECA).	• Used for reviews of mechanical and electrical systems (e.g., fire suppression systems) • Often used to make planned maintenance and equipment inspection plans more effective • Sometimes used to gather information to help find trouble areas in systems
Hazard and Operability (HAZOP) Analysis	The HAZOP analysis technique uses special guide words for (1) suggesting departures from design intents for sections of systems and (2) making sure that the proper safeguards are in place to help prevent system performance problems.	• Used for finding safety hazards and operability problems in continuous process systems, especially fluid and thermal systems. Also used to review procedures and other sequential or batch operations • Another type of guide word analysis technique is Worker and Instruction Safety Evaluation, which is used to understand the significance of human errors
Fault Tree Analysis (FTA)	FTA is a technique that graphically models how logical relationships between equipment failures, human errors, and external events can combine to cause specific accidents of interest. Probabilities and frequencies can be added to the analysis to estimate risks numerically.	• Suited to almost every type of risk assessment, but best used to focus on the basic causes of specific system failures of relatively complex combinations of events • Often used for complex electronic, control, or communication systems • 5 Whys is a less complicated fault tree analysis technique used in incident investigations to determine root causes
Event Tree Analysis (ETA)	ETA is an analysis technique that uses decision trees to model the possible outcomes of an event that can produce an accident of interest. Probabilities and frequencies can be added to the analysis to estimate risks numerically.	• Suited to almost every type of risk assessment, but best used to focus on possible results of events for which many safeguards are in place as protective features • Often used for analysis of facility incidents, the spread of fires or explosions, or toxic releases • A human reliability analysis event tree is a specific and detailed method used in modeling human reliability

Overview of Commonly Used Risk Analysis Tools (continued)

Hazard Risk Analysis Methods	Summary of Method	More Common Uses
Event and Causal Factor Charting	Event and causal factor charting is used to understand how an accident occurred, by finding specific equipment failures, human errors, and external events contributing to the accident. Then, the analysis continues to discover the underlying root causes of the key contributors to the accident and to make recommendations for fixing the root causes.	• Used to study any accident or some selected problem • Event and causal factor charting is most commonly used when the accident scenario is complicated, involving a chain of events or a number of root causes
Preliminary Hazard Analysis (PrHA)	The PrHA technique is a broad, basic study that focuses on (1) finding hazards, (2) assessing the severity of accidents that could occur involving the hazards, and (3) finding protective features or safeguards for reducing the risks of the hazards. This technique focuses on finding weaknesses early in the life of a system, thus saving time and money that might be needed for major redesign if the hazards are found later.	• Usually conducted early in the development of an activity or system when there is little detailed information or few operating procedures, and is often the first of further risk assessments • In any type of system or process, used to identify and rank hazards

Summary of Key Features

Risk Analysis Method	Types of Results				Types of Activities or Systems	Level of Effort/ Complexity	Level of Expertise Required for Analysis Teams
	Qualitative Accident Descriptions	Quantitative Risk Characterizations	Relative Importances of Accident Contributors	Recommendations			
Pareto Analysis		✓	✓	✓	All	Low to medium	Low to medium
Checklist Analysis				✓	All	Low to medium	Low
Relative Ranking/Risk Indexing		✓	✓	✓	All	Low to medium	Low to medium
PrRA	✓	✓	✓	✓	All	Medium	Medium
Change Analysis	✓	✓	✓	✓	All, but generally for systems experiencing recent changes in design or operation	Low to medium	Low to medium
What-if Analysis	✓			✓	All	Medium	Low to medium
FMEA	✓	✓	✓	✓	All, especially mechanical and electrical systems	Medium to high	Medium
HAZOP Analysis	✓			✓	Cargo loading and unloading systems, especially fluid and thermal systems; Sequential operations and procedures	Medium to high	Medium

Summary of Key Features (continued)

Risk Analysis Method	Types of Results				Types of Activities or Systems	Level of Effort/ Complexity	Level of Expertise Required for Analysis Teams
	Qualitative Accident Descriptions	Quantitative Risk Character-izations	Relative Importances of Accident Contributors	Recommendations			
FTA	✓	✓	✓	✓	All	High	Medium to high
ETA	✓	✓	✓	✓	All	High	Medium to high
Event and Causal Factor Charting	✓			✓	All	Low to medium	Low to medium
PrHA	✓	✓		✓	All	Low to medium	Low to medium

Chapter 7
Decision Analysis Tools

1.0 Summary of Decision Analysis Tools

Decision analysis tools provide a structured process for making decisions. This chapter presents four types of decision analysis tools appropriate for many uses:

- Voting methods
- Weighted scoring methods
- Decision trees
- Optimization methods

The following paragraphs describe three basic features of decision analysis tools:

Help structure the decision process. Decision analysis tools have a basic structure to help you examine options and make a decision.

Vary from informal to formal methods. Some tools have very rigid structures, while others are more flexible. Typically, more highly structured tools provide more complete evaluation but often require much more effort than less structured tools. Although less structured tools usually require fewer skills, they need more input from subject matter experts to make up for issues that the decision-making process might overlook. This wide range of methods allows you to choose the proper level of effort for the complexity of the decision.

Provide documentation of the decision-making process. Decision analysis tools provide written data supporting the results of the decision-making process. This documentation can also be used to make other decisions for similar situations.

> ### Guidelines for Selecting Decision Analysis Tools
>
> - **Level of effort**
> - **Uncertainty**
> - **Qualitative or quantitative information**

2.0 Choosing Decision Analysis Tools

A few guidelines should be considered when choosing a decision analysis tool. These include the following:

Level of effort

The amount of time and money spent on decision analysis should depend on the expected results of the decision. Some tools are simple and quick, while others require a lot of effort. For example, a $10,000 decision probably does not warrant a $6,000 decision analysis.

Uncertainty

All data used in the decision-making process will have some level of uncertainty, or doubt. Medium to high levels of uncertainty in the data can produce an uncomfortable level of uncertainty in the analysis results. Some decision analysis tools specifically model uncertainty in the input data.

Qualitative or quantitative information

Most decision analysis tools accept numeric inputs. These inputs range from equipment performance specifications to numerical rankings of features or competing alternatives Some tools handle qualitative inputs (e.g., good reliability, easy to operate, more expensive) more easily than others; however, some tools cannot handle qualitative inputs at all. Most tools provide numeric outputs, such as scoring or ranking of alternatives, for making decisions. The level of detail in the results depends on the complexity of the tool.

Voting Methods

	Results for the Plurality and Ranking Voting Methods								
	Participant					Plurality		Ranking	
Option	A	B	C	D	E	No. of #1 Votes	Position	Average Rank	Position
1	1	1	4	4	5	2	2	3	1
2	8	6	1	1	1	3	1	3.4	3
3	2	4	7	8	3	0		4.8	4
4	7	5	2	7	4	0		5	5
5	3	7	3	5	7	0		5	5
6	6	3	6	6	6	0		5.4	7
7	4	2	5	3	2	0		3.2	2
8	5	8	8	2	8	0		6.2	8

3.0 Summary of Voting Methods

Voting methods for decision analysis use a team of experts to review and vote on different choices. These methods rely on the ability of the stakeholders to understand the advantages and disadvantages of each choice and to vote accordingly.

Brief summary of characteristics

- Minimal effort is required. Modeling of problems requires little information, and the models usually have little structure, with decision factors not plainly identified

- Uncertainty is not specifically modeled but is addressed informally

- Outputs are quantitative

Situations for using voting methods

- Large number of stakeholders

- Possible negative results from the decision are minimal

- Uncertainty and sensitivity analyses are not needed

- Documentation is not required

Advantages of voting methods

- Quick to perform

- Easy to use

- Can be used for almost any decision

Example

The following is a simple example demonstrating the plurality and ranking voting methods. The table below shows the plurality and ranking method used to decide on options 1-4. Each person (A-E) ranked the options in order of preference.

Plurality steps

Results for the Plurality Voting Method							
	Participant					Plurality	
Option	A	B	C	D	E	No. of #1 Votes	Position
Control system 1	1	1	2	2	2	2	2
Control system 2	4	3	1	1	1	3	1
Control system 3	2	4	3	3	3	0	
Control system 4	3	2	4	4	4	0	

Step 1. Each person ranks the alternatives. The table shows that Options 1 and 2 received all of the first phase votes.

Step 2. Select the alternative with the most #1 votes. Option 2 is selected using the plurality method.

Ranking steps

Results for the Ranking Voting Method							
	Participant					Ranking	
Option	A	B	C	D	E	Average Rank	Position
Control system 1	1	1	2	2	2	1.6	1
Control system 2	4	3	1	1	1	2.0	2
Control system 3	2	4	3	3	3	3.0	3
Control system 4	3	2	4	4	4	3.4	4

Step 1. Each participant ranks all alternatives. The rows of numbers under participants A - E show the ranking of each option by each participant.

Step 2. The rankings are summed and averaged. The average rank column shows the average ranking of each option.

Step 3. The alternative with the lowest average is selected.

Option 1 is chosen using the ranking method as shown by the position column.

Disadvantages of voting methods

- When voting methods are used, there is usually very little written data to show how a decision was reached. This can lead to second-guessing of the decision, especially by individuals outside the voting group. Lack of documentation limits the ability to use the information in making other, similar decisions.

- Voting methods often do not make use of all information available to the decision-making group. For example, the plurality method does not consider the ranking of options, and neither the ranking method nor the plurality method considers the way an individual prefers one option over another.

- Strengths and weaknesses of options are unclear. The negative aspects of an alternative are usually not described, and the reasons for supporting an option are not documented.

- Typically, the issues or options are only listed and not described. This can lead to confusion as to what is really being voted on.

- The information from each expert is typically weighted equally, regardless of the actual experience of each expert.

4.0 Summary of Weighted Scoring Methods

Weighted scoring methods plainly identify decision factors, and each alternative is compared to the factors. The decision models address many factors. A numerical value is assigned to each alternative for each factor. Various factors are weighted differently. The weighted numerical values are added, and the alternative with the highest score is the best overall alternative.

Brief summary of characteristics

- Both qualitative and quantitative inputs are easily handled
- Each alternative is given an overall score

Situations for using weighted scoring methods

- Group or individual decision making
- Few alternatives (<10)
- Timing is not an issue

Example

The following example demonstrates the steps for using a weighted scoring method to make decisions. The decision involves choosing a fuel pump.

Weighted Scoring Steps

Step 1. Define the decision factors of interest. For choosing a fuel pump, the following factors should be considered:

- Safety
- Flowrate (i.e., capacity)
- Cost (initial and operating

Step 2. Assign importance levels, or weights, to each decision factor. Weight each decision factor based on its importance in the decision-making process. Subject matter experts need to participate in this step.

Factor	Weight
Safety	30%
Flowrate	20%
Cost	50%
	100%

Step 3. Develop scales for changing decision factor values into scores.

A scale of some type allows the decision maker to rate the factors of each option. Scales can be created in a variety of forms. The following are scales for cost, safety, and flowrate.

Evaluation scale for cost

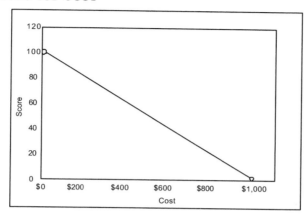

Evaluation scale for safety

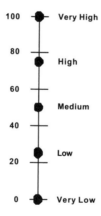

Evaluation scale for flowrate

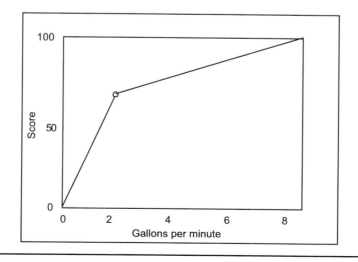

Decision Analysis Tools

Step 4. Score each decision for each alternative, multiply the score by its weight, and sum the weighted scores. The table below shows the ratings of four pumps. For example, Pump D has a medium safety (which translates to a 50), a flowrate of 2.1 gallons per minute (which translates to 70.5), and a cost of $400 (which translates to 60). The weighted scores are the weights of each factor multiplied by the score.

Factor		Value (Score)				Weighted Scores			
	Weight	Pump A	Pump B	Pump C	Pump D	Pump A	Pump B	Pump C	Pump D
Safety	30%	Very High (100)	High (75)	Medium (50)	Medium (50)	30	22.5	15	15
Flowrate	20%	2.6 (73)	2.5 (72.5)	1.3 (45.5)	2.1 (70.5)	14.6	14.5	9.1	14.1
Cost	50%	$520 (48)	$270 (73)	$560 (44)	$400 (60)	24	36.5	22	30
Initial		$500	$230	$430	$350				
Operating		$20	$40	$130	$50				
					Total	68.6	**73.5**	46.1	59.1

Advantages of weighted scoring methods

- Address different factors
- Different types of scales can be used for the various factors
- Decision factors are plainly identified and weighted so the group can reach an agreement on each item
- Can be used by individuals or groups

Disadvantages of weighted scoring methods

- Time consuming — decision factors and evaluation scales must be developed, and each alternative must be compared against each evaluation scale
- Basic scoring models do not plainly account for uncertainty
- Difficult to address future events or pending decisions
- Decision factors may be linked, which may result in double counting.

5.0 Summary of Decision Trees

The decision tree method of decision analysis uses a tree structure to illustrate the decision process. Probabilities are assigned to events, and the expected value of each alternative is determined. The alternative with the most attractive total expected value is chosen. Depending on the decision, the most attractive expected value may be the highest or lowest number.

Brief summary of characteristics

- Decision trees require (1) sequential modeling of decision points and chance events and (2) the development of probabilities and outcome values for each branch

- Uncertainty of inputs is plainly modeled in the tree branches

- Sensitivity analysis can be implemented easily but is best approached with commercial software

- Inputs and outputs are quantitative. Qualitative inputs are difficult to address.

Situations for using decision trees

- Sequential decision models

- Uncertain inputs

Advantages of decision trees

- Can be used to show a series of conditional choices

- Can be used to show the impact of time on decisions

- Can plainly model uncertainty

- Can produce quantitative results

Disadvantages of decision trees

- All decision factors must be changed into common units. Qualitative inputs may be difficult to convert (e.g., translating community goodwill to dollars, or effects on organizational reputation to dollars)

- Decision trees are harder to develop in a group setting

- Developing and reaching agreement on event probabilities may be difficult

- Qualitative methods are not easily used

- The number of possible outcomes in the model can be extremely large

5.1 Application of the Decision Tree Method
What is the best way to get to work?

Below is a graphical representation of the decision and possible outcomes.

Decision	Alternatives		Uncertainties		Outcomes	Values	Utility
	Transportation Mode		Traffic Congestion	Prob.	Commute Time		
	Drive	Route A	Light	0.3		Total Cost	
How should I get to work tomorrow?		Route B	Medium	0.2			U (total cost)
	Ride the Train		Heavy	0.5	Commute Cost		

First, calculate the cost (or total cost of each possible outcome.

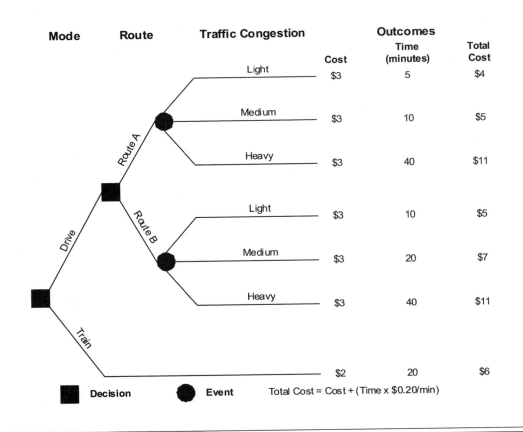

				Cost	Outcomes Time (minutes)	Total Cost
Mode	Route	Traffic Congestion				
	Route A	Light		$3	5	$4
		Medium		$3	10	$5
		Heavy		$3	40	$11
Drive	Route B	Light		$3	10	$5
		Medium		$3	20	$7
		Heavy		$3	40	$11
Train				$2	20	$6

■ Decision   ● Event   Total Cost = Cost + (Time x $0.20/min)

Next, calculate the expected cost of each outcome and the total expected cost of each alternative (route).

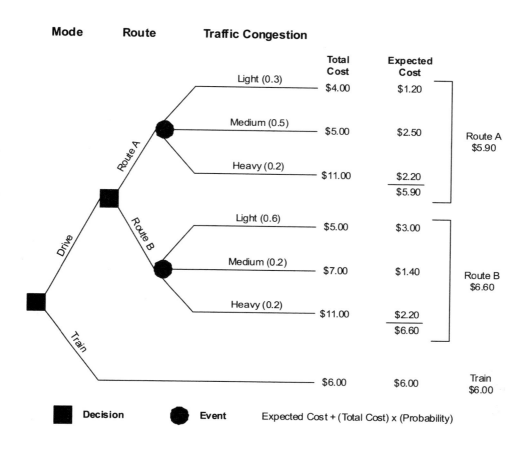

Mode   **Route**   **Traffic Congestion**

	Total Cost	Expected Cost	

Light (0.3) — $4.00 — $1.20

Medium (0.5) — $5.00 — $2.50

Heavy (0.2) — $11.00 — $2.20 / $5.90 — Route A $5.90

Light (0.6) — $5.00 — $3.00

Medium (0.2) — $7.00 — $1.40

Heavy (0.2) — $11.00 — $2.20 / $6.60 — Route B $6.60

Train — $6.00 — $6.00 — Train $6.00

■ **Decision**   ● **Event**   Expected Cost + (Total Cost) x (Probability)

Decision Analysis Tools

If desired, multiple events can be analyzed and chained together. The case below considers the traffic report (which could be in error) for each driving alternative. The resulting decision tree would look like the one below. The tables on the following pages calculate the expected values of the alternatives.

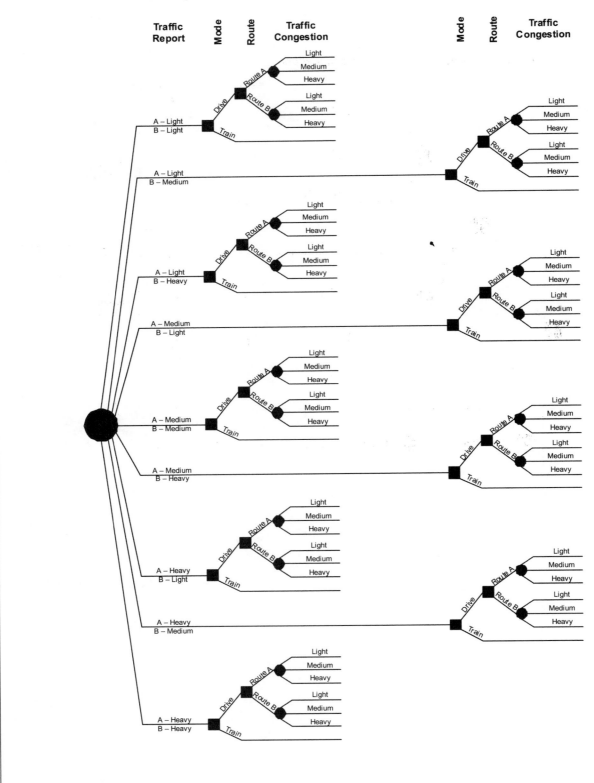

A	B	Mode	Route	Actual Congestion	Listen to Traffic Report	Travel Time	Parking/ Fare	Time	Total Cost	Probability	Expected Cost	Group Expected Cost
Light	Light	Drive	A	Light	5	5	$3.00	$2.00	$5.00	0.90	$4.50	
		Drive	A	Medium	5	10	$3.00	$3.00	$6.00	0.00	$0.00	$5.70
		Drive	A	Heavy	5	40	$3.00	$9.00	$12.00	0.10	$1.20	
		Drive	B	Light	5	10	$3.00	$3.00	$6.00	0.90	$5.40	
		Drive	B	Medium	5	20	$3.00	$5.00	$8.00	0.00	$0.00	$6.60
		Drive	B	Heavy	5	40	$3.00	$9.00	$12.00	0.10	$1.20	
		Train			5	20	$2.00	$5.00	$7.00	1.00	$7.00	$7.00
Light	Medium	Drive	A	Light	5	5	$3.00	$2.00	$5.00	0.90	$4.50	
		Drive	A	Medium	5	10	$3.00	$3.00	$6.00	0.00	$0.00	$5.70
		Drive	A	Heavy	5	40	$3.00	$9.00	$12.00	0.10	$1.20	
		Drive	B	Light	5	10	$3.00	$3.00	$6.00	0.10	$0.60	
		Drive	B	Medium	5	20	$3.00	$5.00	$8.00	0.80	$6.40	$8.20
		Drive	B	Heavy	5	40	$3.00	$9.00	$12.00	0.10	$1.20	
		Train			5	20	$2.00	$5.00	$7.00	1.00	$7.00	$7.00
Light	Heavy	Drive	A	Light	5	5	$3.00	$2.00	$5.00	0.90	$4.50	
		Drive	A	Medium	5	10	$3.00	$3.00	$6.00	0.00	$0.00	$5.70
		Drive	A	Heavy	5	40	$3.00	$9.00	$12.00	0.10	$1.20	
		Drive	B	Light	5	10	$3.00	$3.00	$6.00	0.00	$0.00	
		Drive	B	Medium	5	20	$3.00	$5.00	$8.00	0.15	$1.20	$11.40
		Drive	B	Heavy	5	40	$3.00	$9.00	$12.00	0.85	$10.20	
		Train			5	20	$2.00	$5.00	$7.00	1.00	$7.00	$7.00
Medium	Light	Drive	A	Light	5	5	$3.00	$2.00	$5.00	0.15	$0.75	
		Drive	A	Medium	5	10	$3.00	$3.00	$6.00	0.70	$4.20	$6.75
		Drive	A	Heavy	5	40	$3.00	$9.00	$12.00	0.15	$1.80	
		Drive	B	Light	5	10	$3.00	$3.00	$6.00	0.90	$5.40	
		Drive	B	Medium	5	20	$3.00	$5.00	$8.00	0.00	$0.00	$6.60
		Drive	B	Heavy	5	40	$3.00	$9.00	$12.00	0.10	$1.20	
		Train			5	20	$2.00	$5.00	$7.00	1.00	$7.00	$7.00
Medium	Medium	Drive	A	Light	5	5	$3.00	$2.00	$5.00	0.15	$0.75	
		Drive	A	Medium	5	10	$3.00	$3.00	$6.00	0.70	$4.20	$6.75
		Drive	A	Heavy	5	40	$3.00	$9.00	$12.00	0.15	$1.80	
		Drive	B	Light	5	10	$3.00	$3.00	$6.00	0.10	$0.60	
		Drive	B	Medium	5	20	$3.00	$5.00	$8.00	0.80	$6.40	$8.20
		Drive	B	Heavy	5	40	$3.00	$9.00	$12.00	0.10	$1.20	
		Train			5	20	$2.00	$5.00	$7.00	1.00	$7.00	$7.00

A	B	Mode	Route	Actual Congestion	Listen to Traffic Report	Travel Time	Parking/ Fare	Time	Total Cost	Probability	Expected Cost	Group Expected Cost
Medium	Heavy	Drive	A	Light	5	5	$3.00	$2.00	$5.00	0.15	$0.75	
		Drive	A	Medium	5	10	$3.00	$3.00	$6.00	0.70	$4.20	$6.75
		Drive	A	Heavy	5	40	$3.00	$9.00	$12.00	0.15	$1.80	
		Drive	B	Light	5	10	$3.00	$3.00	$6.00	0.00	$0.00	
		Drive	B	Medium	5	20	$3.00	$5.00	$8.00	0.15	$1.20	$11.40
		Drive	B	Heavy	5	40	$3.00	$9.00	$12.00	0.85	$10.20	
		Train			5	20	$2.00	$5.00	$7.00	1.00	$7.00	$7.00
Heavy	Light	Drive	A	Light	5	5	$3.00	$2.00	$5.00	0.00	$0.00	
		Drive	A	Medium	5	10	$3.00	$3.00	$6.00	0.20	$1.20	$10.80
		Drive	A	Heavy	5	40	$3.00	$9.00	$12.00	0.80	$9.60	
		Drive	B	Light	5	10	$3.00	$3.00	$6.00	0.90	$5.40	
		Drive	B	Medium	5	20	$3.00	$5.00	$8.00	0.00	$0.00	$6.60
		Drive	B	Heavy	5	40	$3.00	$9.00	$12.00	0.10	$1.20	
		Train			5	20	$2.00	$5.00	$7.00	1.00	$7.00	$7.00
Heavy	Medium	Drive	A	Light	5	5	$3.00	$2.00	$5.00	0.00	$0.00	
		Drive	A	Medium	5	10	$3.00	$3.00	$6.00	0.20	$1.20	$10.80
		Drive	A	Heavy	5	40	$3.00	$9.00	$12.00	0.80	$9.60	
		Drive	B	Light	5	10	$3.00	$3.00	$6.00	0.10	$0.60	
		Drive	B	Medium	5	20	$3.00	$5.00	$8.00	0.80	$6.40	$8.20
		Drive	B	Heavy	5	40	$3.00	$9.00	$12.00	0.10	$1.20	
		Train			5	20	$2.00	$5.00	$7.00	1.00	$7.00	$7.00
Heavy	Heavy	Drive	A	Light	5	5	$3.00	$2.00	$5.00	0.00	$0.00	
		Drive	A	Medium	5	10	$3.00	$3.00	$6.00	0.20	$1.20	$10.80
		Drive	A	Heavy	5	40	$3.00	$9.00	$12.00	0.80	$9.60	
		Drive	B	Light	5	10	$3.00	$3.00	$6.00	0.00	$0.00	
		Drive	B	Medium	5	20	$3.00	$5.00	$8.00	0.15	$1.20	$11.40
		Drive	B	Heavy	5	40	$3.00	$9.00	$12.00	0.85	$10.20	
		Train			5	20	$2.00	$5.00	$7.00	1.00	$7.00	$7.00

> **Other Decision Analysis Tools**
>
> ■ **Optimization Methods**
> ■ **Kepner**
> ■ **Benefit-cost Analysis**
> ■ **Multiattribute Utility Analysis**

6.0 Other Decision Analysis Tools

There are other decision analysis tools available, and some are listed below. Those included in this chapter were chosen because they are well developed, widely usable, and cover a range of complexity.

Optimization Methods

- Can address many or infinite alternatives

- Accept only quantitative inputs

- Find the optimal solution to a complex problem

- Identify feasible solutions that meet all limits

- Require a great deal of effort to develop and solve equations. Reaching stakeholder agreement on the model may be difficult.

- Uncertainty is not directly addressed

Kepner-Tregoe Decision Analysis

Similar to the weighted scoring method, but evaluation scales are not developed

Uncertainty not directly addressed

Benefit-cost Analysis

Tries to make decisions independent of the preferences of decision makers

Is data driven

Minimizes the cost/benefit ratio across the affected groups

Group that pays for the analysis may not receive benefits

Often used by government agencies

Multiattribute Utility Analysis

Extension of decision analysis and decision trees to address more than one performance criterion

Plainly addresses uncertainty and value trade-offs

Evaluation scales much the same as weighted scoring methods developed

Chapter 8

Managing a Risk Assessment Project

Overview of Risk Assessment Project Management

Selecting the right approach and tools for your application is important, but it does not guarantee success. In fact, the way you implement an approach generally has more influence on your ultimate success than the approach itself. For example, an expert craftsman can often accomplish more with rudimentary tools than a novice can with even the most sophisticated power tools. To help ensure a successful risk assessment, it is important to perform several activities related to managing the project. This chapter discusses these project management steps, as shown above, and their importance to the success of the risk assessment.

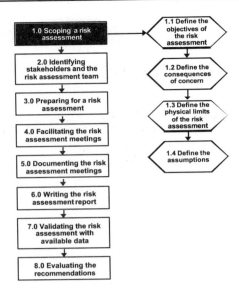

1.0 Scoping a Risk Assessment

Defining the scope of a risk assessment is critical to success. A lack of clear direction can waste time and resources, causing the team to examine issues of relatively minor interest or concern.

The scope provides the boundaries necessary to focus the risk assessment objectives. However, it is important that the scope not be defined so restrictively that it stifles the risk assessment team. The team must have the latitude to exercise good judgment in the investigation of issues initially outside the scope. Fundamentally, the risk assessment should be scoped to address the issues at the highest level possible while still satisfying the necessary objectives.

Following are the major choices that define the scope of any risk assessment:

1.1 Define the objectives of the risk assessment

- Determine the motivation for performing the risk assessment. This may include management concern, unit concern, public concern, or regulatory compliance
- Determine the operating modes to be considered
- Develop a *wish list* of information desired from the risk assessment

1.2 Define the consequences of concern

- Public injury
- Personnel injury
- Equipment or property damage
- Environmental damage
- Revenue loss
- Community relations

1.3 Define the physical limits of the risk assessment

The physical limits of the risk assessment include the breadth and depth of the risk assessment, the uncertainty of results, and the availability of resources.

Breadth of risk assessment. This issue focuses on what is to be analyzed. If overall risk-related information for an activity or system is needed, the risk assessment scope should include all associated operations or subsystems. For example, a risk assessment might ask, "What is the total risk of contained operations?" However, if information needs are restricted to specific functions or components, a narrow focus on that equipment is appropriate. Such a focus might ask the question, "What is the risk associated with the boom crane?" The breadth of risk assessment should be as narrow as possible without overlooking potentially important contributors to activity or system performance. For example, if an emergency shutdown system were an issue, a risk assessment would typically need to focus both on the components of that system and its interfaces with other systems.

Depth of risk assessment. This issue focuses on the level of resolution within the risk assessment. That is, "How detailed an evaluation is required for each entity within the breadth of risk assessment?" Risk assessments should generally be performed in stages, progressing one level at a time. For example, an overall activity assessment would be performed at an operation level. The operation contributing most of the potential problems could then be assessed in more detail, if more detailed information were judged to be beneficial to decision makers. This process would be repeated in assessing important operations at the function level, important functions at the component level, etc. This concept can be considered a hierarchy.

- ∅ Overall Activity
  - ∅ Operations
    - ∅ Functions
      - ∅ Components

A progressive level of resolution that focuses on the most significant areas produces an efficient risk assessment, without overworking problems.

Uncertainty of results. This issue focuses on the level of confidence that decision makers require from risk assessment results. Very detailed numerical estimates characterizing expected risk are sometimes necessary. These numerical estimates often include statistical confidence bounds. However, subjective, qualitative judgments about expected risk are tolerable for many risk assessments. Of course, various levels of risk assessment between these extremes are possible, including categorization methods. The need for greater certainty is generally associated with the following:

1. **More severe consequences if systems are unreliable.** If a specific human error or equipment failure could result in a catastrophic accident, as opposed to only a minor inconvenience, then the risk assessment may need to be more refined.

2. Lack of familiarity or experience with new systems. Risk assessments of new designs are often more detailed and systematic than those of activities and systems that have been performed successfully for many years.

3. Requirements for demonstrating compliance with numerical goals. Risk assessments demonstrating that components can achieve specific risk goals would require a more precise study than those for qualitatively identifying failure modes.

Using the highest tolerable level of uncertainty that does not affect decision making minimizes risk assessment burdens without compromising results.

A risk analyst must be open and honest about any assumptions made in scoping the risk assessment and the degree of uncertainty expected in the results. These assumptions and expected uncertainties in results must be captured in the risk assessment project so that (1) the decision maker can use them as factors in his or her final decision and (2) they can serve as points from which future, similar risk assessments can be validated.

Availability of resources. This issue focuses on what type of risk assessment is feasible, given limited time, money, and personnel resources. A surplus of resources is not a reason to perform more analysis than necessary; however, inadequate resources may necessitate a more restrictive scope than would have been selected otherwise.

1.4 Define the assumptions

Clearly defined assumptions help ensure a consistent risk assessment. Here are some typical assumptions:

- Equipment is fit for its intended use
- Trained personnel will be used
- Written procedures are accurate
- Policies are enforced

In summary

In scoping a risk assessment, it is best to make the assessment the minimum necessary to satisfy its objectives. In other words, aim for a risk assessment that addresses the issue at the highest level possible, tolerating the most possible uncertainty and using the fewest possible resources.

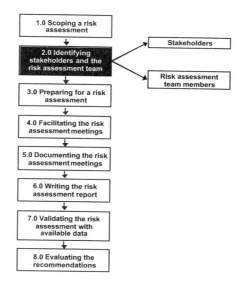

2.0 Identifying Stakeholders and the Risk Assessment Team

Stakeholders

There are five types of individuals or groups who participate in the risk assessment process:

Sponsor — This individual or group determines the need for the particular risk assessment. The sponsor is ultimately responsible for obtaining results from the risk assessment and typically has a specific use for the results.

Analyst — This individual or group, such as a risk specialist, is responsible for performing the risk assessment.

Subject matter experts — This group participates in the risk assessment, providing expert knowledge and experience about relevant operations, configurations, and potential problems. It may include unit staff and outside experts.

Decision maker — This individual or group uses the risk assessment process results to make risk-based decisions. The decision maker is often the sponsor.

Others affected by the decision — This group can include internal or external organizations as well as individuals who will likely be affected by the risk-based decision. This group should be appropriately represented throughout the risk assessment process.

Risk assessment team members

The risk assessment team consists of **analysts** and **subject matter experts**. Risk assessments are sometimes performed solely by analysts in a one-person team, but the best risk assessments always involve activity and system experts.

Following is a more detailed description of the risk assessment team members:

Analysts — *act as either team leaders or scribes*

Team leader — *organizes and facilitates the analysis*

Characteristics:

- Independent of subject activity or system; not the activity or system expert
- Able to organize and negotiate
- Communicates well with a diverse group
- Can focus group energy and build consensus
- Impartial, honest, and ethical
- Experienced with risk analysis techniques

Scribe — *records the proceedings of the analysis in an orderly manner*

Characteristics:

- Attentive to detail
- Able to organize
- Understands technical terminology
- Able to summarize discussions
- Good writing and typing skills
- Understands the risk assessment techniques

Subject matter experts — *postulate causes, estimate consequences, identify safeguards, and suggest ways to address unacceptable loss exposures*

Characteristics:

- Enter into the discussion enthusiastically
- Contribute their experience
- Confine the discussion to the specific problem
- Listen attentively to the discussion
- Appreciate other team members' points of view

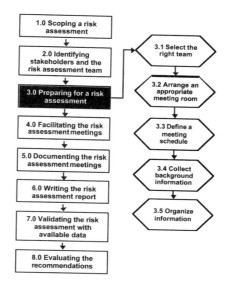

3.0 Preparing for a Risk Assessment

Preparing for a risk assessment is as crucial as performing the assessment. Poor preparation can undermine the analysis. The analysts and sponsor should work together to ensure that the risk assessment runs smoothly.

3.1 Select the right team

- Choose an appropriate number of team members. This is often three to six for team-based approaches.

- Appoint team members with a variety of experience and expertise

- Ensure that team members are objective

- Consider and balance the personality traits of individuals on the team; avoid disruptive people

- Balance the positions of the individuals on the team; managers and officers may intimidate some individuals, keeping them from contributing

- Consider the impact on operations

3.2 Arrange an appropriate meeting room

- Verify that the room is large enough to accommodate the team members

- Ensure that seating arrangements are comfortable

- Consider using an onsite location that accommodates tours and inspections; an offsite location may be necessary if team members are likely to be interrupted or called out during the analysis

- Consider using a room near restrooms and refreshments if possible

- Avoid distractions such as phones, loud speakers, other noises, etc.

3.3 Define a meeting schedule

- Meetings should not exceed four to six hours per day

- Risk assessment meetings should not last more than four or five days in a row. Large analyses will typically meet every two or three weeks.

- Schedule ample time to document the risk assessment, resolve the recommendations, and conduct a high-level benefit-cost analysis on the recommendations

- Distribute meeting schedules early enough for team members to arrange their own schedules

3.4 Collect background information

Collect appropriate drawings, procedures, policies, etc., that would be useful as references during the risk assessment.

If appropriate, develop other information collection methods, such as written surveys, and obtain the results for the risk assessment. Surveys and other statistical methods to obtain reference data should be developed with expert assistance.

3.5 Organize information

Prepare documentation tools such as worksheets or software — Whether paper or software is used to document the risk assessment, the documentation tools need to be prepared in advance.

Gather and distribute information on the subject to be assessed — The team leader should gather all appropriate drawings, procedures, policies, etc., that may be necessary for reference during the risk assessment. If appropriate, this information can be distributed to the team members before the risk assessment for their review.

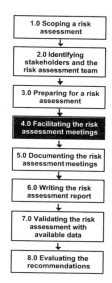

4.0 Facilitating the Risk Assessment Meetings

The team leader facilitates the analysis meeting. Proper organization and facilitation make the risk assessment run smoothly and promote an environment conducive to meeting its objectives. Below are some facilitation tips and issues to consider.

General meeting guidelines

- Introduce the team members
- Review the problem scope and objectives
- Define ground rules for the meeting, such as equality of team members, no problem solving
- Discuss the meeting schedule
- Perform the risk assessment section by section
- Review results with the team

Questioning techniques for the analysis

- Ask nonthreatening questions:

    "What factors do you emphasize when training new personnel?"

    or

    "What kinds of problems have you seen?"

    not

    "What kinds of mistakes have you made?"

- Treat team members as experts
- Solicit details of past accidents, and ask if similar situations could recur
- Direct questions to the quiet team members
- Confine yourself to asking questions, not providing answers

Keys to a successful meeting

- Listen to all team members
- Promote participation; avoid criticism
- Take frequent breaks to keep energy level high, and limit meetings to four to six hours per day
- Identify ultimate causes and consequences of deviations
- Keep the meeting moving forward

Common meeting problems to avoid

- Out-of-date documentation
- Ill-defined design intentions and functions
- Inadequate information to understand the problem
- Sidetracked discussions
- Digressing into designing solutions

Follow-up activities

- Identify all open items (i.e., unanswered questions) that must be resolved
- Assign a person and schedule for each open item
- Review all recommendations with the team
- Schedule additional meetings as necessary

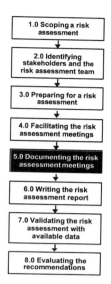

5.0 Documenting the Risk Assessment Meetings

Each risk assessment technique has its own method for collecting, organizing, and reporting data. All of these techniques can be performed using paper-based worksheets or electronic software tools, either general purpose software or technique-specific tools.

Regardless of the method used to document the analysis, the team leader and scribe should be familiar with the tools and be able to explain the documentation process to the other team members.

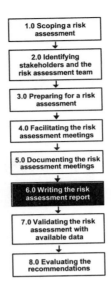

6.0 Writing the Risk Assessment Report

Documentation of the risk assessment results accomplishes the following:

- Provides evidence that the study was performed using sound practices

- Preserves the results for future use

- Supports other activities, such as procedures, training, and accident investigation

- Supports good management decisions

Documentation requirements should be defined before the risk assessment is performed to ensure that the proper information is collected. Below is a list of the key topics that would be included in a report:

- What was analyzed?

- Which risk assessment technique was used?

- How were the regulatory or internal requirements met?

- Who performed the risk assessment?

- What were the action items?

- What was management's response?

The following page is an example outline of a risk assessment report. Reports may be more general or more specific than this outline, depending on the intended audience and use of the documentation.

Abstract

Summary

Table of Contents

List of Tables

List of Figures

1.0 Introduction

2.0 Activity Overview

3.0 Risk Assessment Approach

   3.1 Composition of the Team

   3.2 Brief Description of the Risk Assessment Techniques Used (e.g., Preliminary Risk Analysis, Fault Tree Analysis, What-if Analysis, etc.)

   3.3 Specific Risk Assessment Issues

      3.3.1 Problems of Interest

      3.3.2 History of Problems

      3.3.3 Other Issues

4.0 Risk Assessment Results

   4.1 Risk-related Information

   4.2 Recommendations

   4.3 Concluding Remarks

Appendix A: Risk Assessment Documentation (e.g., analysis worksheets, job aids created)

Appendix B: Report Reference Material

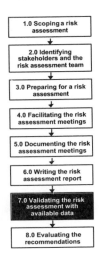

7.0 Validating the Risk Assessment with Available Data

Once the risk assessment is complete, it should be validated in areas where applicable data are available. Two types of data are helpful for validating a risk assessment: historical data and similar risk assessments.

Historical data

Care should be taken when using historical data, such as accident statistics and past equipment failure rates. A risk assessment is used to understand future loss performance and is based on current and anticipated future operating parameters for the system. Historical data is based on past operating conditions and generally reflects a short period of time, relative to the expected frequency of recurrence for most accident scenarios. When using historical data to validate a risk assessment, be sure to understand operating conditions from the past and apply them properly to results from the risk assessment.

Similar risk assessments

Similar risk assessments have sometimes already been conducted. These are helpful for understanding how other teams approached a risk-based decision-making application and how they evaluated the risk of similar scenarios. When using other risk assessments to validate an analysis, the context of the other risk assessments must be fully understood.

Risk assessment validation process

Though the following validation process can be streamlined, a standard risk assessment validation flow chart is presented on the next page. This process provides a review of all aspects of the risk assessment process and results. The validation process is designed to provide the following:

- Review of the composition of the risk assessment team

- Review of the team's performance of the risk assessment process

- Review of the risk assessment results and data

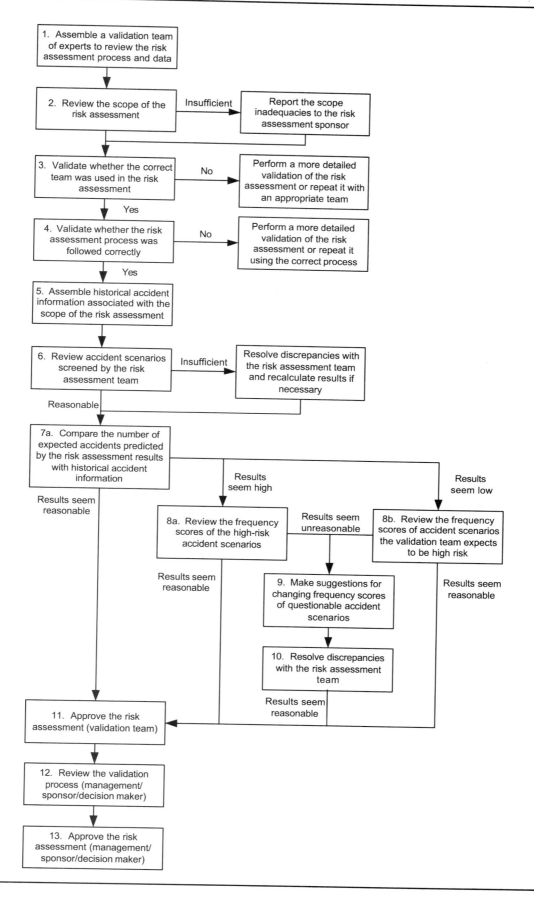

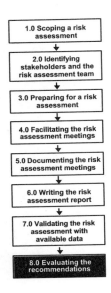

1.0 Scoping a risk assessment

2.0 Identifying stakeholders and the risk assessment team

3.0 Preparing for a risk assessment

4.0 Facilitating the risk assessment meetings

5.0 Documenting the risk assessment meetings

6.0 Writing the risk assessment report

7.0 Validating the risk assessment with available data

8.0 Evaluating the recommendations

8.0 Evaluating the Recommendations

The following flowchart illustrates a logical management process for evaluating recommendations.

Ideally, all recommendations from risk assessments would be (1) the most effective and efficient way of meeting the risk-related goals for the subject activity or system and (2) implemented in a timely manner.

However, this may not be the case for some of the following reasons:

- Better improvement options than those generated through the risk assessments are sometimes available

  Recommendations could sometimes inadvertently do more harm than good

  Implementation of good ideas must be delayed to allow adequate preparation time or to secure additional implementation resources

Management should therefore review the recommendations from risk assessments carefully before deciding to implement them. Management should then ensure that adopted recommendations are implemented in a timely manner. Timely resolution is important because unresolved recommendations can lead to (1) accidents from the problems they were intended to address and (2) legal or regulatory problems if major accidents occur that the recommendations could have helped prevent.

Examples of reasons for rejecting a recommendation

- A detailed engineering analysis following the risk assessment indicated that the suggestion was not a good idea because . . .

Other information not available to the analysts indicates that the potential problem is not as significant as the analysis results indicate.

The situation has changed; the recommendation is no longer valid because . . .

Implementation of other recommendations makes this action no longer necessary.

The recommendation, although somewhat beneficial, does not provide as much benefit as . . .

The cost of implementing the recommendation is not justified in light of the anticipated benefit.

Before implementing a recommendation, a benefit-cost analysis should be performed to determine if it is worthwhile. The following paragraphs discuss methods for estimating the benefit and cost of a recommendation and determining the benefit-cost ratio.

Benefit

Estimate the benefit of a recommendation by determining the following:

Expected cost of accidents if the recommendation is not implemented

MINUS

Expected cost of accidents after the recommendation is implemented

Revised costs are generally assessed for accidents by changing the risk assessment inputs (failure logic, failure rates, repair rates, etc.) to reflect expected conditions after the recommendation is implemented. In detailed assessments of recommendations, the time when benefits are realized (e.g., only after five years) may be important because of the time value of money.

Cost

Estimate the costs of implementing a recommendation by considering the total life cycle costs of the change:

Initial implementation cost (design, equipment, installation, training, etc.)

PLUS

Annual costs for ongoing implementation (utilities, maintenance and testing, etc.)

In detailed assessments, the time when costs are realized may be important because of the time value of money.

Benefit-cost ratio

Calculate the benefit-cost ratio by dividing the benefit derived from the recommendation by the cost of implementing it. The following figure is a simple illustration of benefit-cost ratios. Implement recommendations with the largest benefit-cost ratios first, unless (1) the cumulative benefit of implementing several lower-cost items provides a more attractive return on investment or (2) the resources are simply not available to implement relatively expensive items, even if the benefits are substantial.

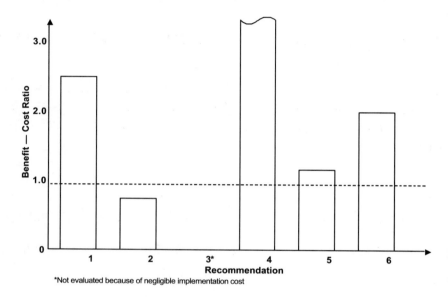

*Not evaluated because of negligible implementation cost

A benefit-cost ratio of less than 1 indicates that the recommendation is undesirable.

For relatively inexpensive items that seem reasonable, management will often decide to implement the recommendations without detailed benefit-cost analysis because the cost of detailed analysis may be comparable to the cost of implementation.

9.0 Reviewing a Risk Assessment

At some time, you may have to review a risk assessment that has been conducted by other personnel or organizations. The purpose of this section is to provide guidelines for reviewing risk assessments conducted by others. You might also find it valuable to apply these review criteria to your own risk assessments. These criteria are consistent with those applied by the National Research Council to risk assessments during peer reviews.

The intent of this section is NOT to provide you with a checklist for evaluating each type of risk assessment tool; rather, it is to offer guidelines for reviewing any risk assessment using any tool.

The evaluation should cover four areas:

- Scope

- Data collection

- Data analysis

- Recommendations and conclusions

9.1 Scope

The scope of a risk assessment includes the decision framework and the physical and analytical boundaries of the risk assessment.

Review questions

1. **Has the purpose of the risk assessment been clearly defined?** This should include a definition of the decision that needs to be made, the questions that must be answered to make the decision, and the type, precision, and certainty of the information necessary to answer the questions. Once the purpose of the risk assessment has been verified, the rest of the review will focus on judging how well the risk assessment process fulfills its purpose.

2. **Are the boundaries of the risk assessments defined?** Specific boundaries of the analysis are sometimes established. For the purposes of a review, the key is to be sure that established constraints are (1) consistent with the purpose of the analysis (e.g., critical issues are not being ignored) and (2) appropriately observed by the analysis team.

9.2 Data collection

Data include both qualitative and quantitative information collected and analyzed during an assessment. It is essential to understand how data were collected for the risk assessment. The data collection methods should be clearly defined and defended in the risk assessment report.

Review questions

1. **Were appropriate data collected for the risk assessments?**

   Ask the following:

   - Did the risk assessment team develop the types of information needed by the decision makers?

   - Is each type of information presented with the precision and certainty required by decision makers?

   - Was an appropriate process used to gather and elicit the data dependably?

   - Were skilled individuals used to facilitate the data collection process?

2. **Were data collected from the best sources?**

   Ask the following:

   - Were appropriate subject matter experts involved throughout the risk assessment?

   - Were appropriate databases used to collect historical experience data?

   - Were the databases used appropriately?

3. **Are raw data included in the risk assessment report, or are they otherwise available?**

   The raw data should be included as an appendix, or should be available in some form, so that the logical progression from data collection to data analysis to recommendations and conclusions is verifiable.

9.3 Data analysis

Once the data are collected, they must be analyzed so that proper conclusions can be drawn. As with data collection, the data analysis methods should be clearly defined and defended.

Review questions

1. **Was the data analysis performed competently?** The answer to this question is based on the experience and skill of the analysts as well as whether the analysts used established and accepted methods.

2. **Is it easy to see how the collected data were analyzed?** The reviewer should be able to easily see how the collected data were treated during the data analysis process. For example, raw data may be itemized on a table. The item numbers are then transferred to the data analysis component of the risk assessment to show how and where the raw data were actually analyzed. Also, data simulations may be used, and the impact from these simulations should be clear.

3. **Are the actual results from the data analysis presented clearly?** Often, large amounts of data are analyzed in a risk assessment. To ensure that the proper recommendations are presented and appropriate conclusions are drawn, the results of the data analysis should be presented in a tabular, matrix, or other summary format. The recommendations and conclusions can then be derived and defended from these summary results.

9.4 Recommendations and conclusions

A risk assessment is not complete if it does not contain recommendations and conclusions. Recommendations are made by the analysis team to improve the risk performance. The conclusions are an interpretation of the results of the data analysis. Conclusions are often made about the overall acceptability of risk. They also include other key observations about the risks, such as contributions, costs, vulnerable populations, etc.

Review questions

1. **Is it easy to see how the recommendations and conclusions were made?** The reviewer should be able to easily see how the results from the data analysis were used to generate recommendations and conclusions. Recommendations and conclusions should be defended based on the data analysis results.

2. **Do the conclusions answer the questions from which the risk-based decisions will be made?** If the conclusions do not tie in with the purpose of the analysis, then the risk assessment did not meet its main objective.

3. **Were sensitive policy issues treated with proper care?** Some recommendations and conclusions may be inflammatory to some audiences and should be worded appropriately.

4. **Was the organization of the report effective?** The report itself should clearly lead readers from the scope of the risk assessment through the recommendations and conclusion without the need for additional supporting materials, explanations or presentations.

Appendix A
Table for Applying the Risk-Based Decision Making Process

Step 1: Establish the Decision Structure	
Step 1a: Define the decision	
Description: Specifically describe what decision(s) must be made. Major categories of decisions include (1) accepting or rejecting a proposed facility or operation, (2) determining who and what to inspect, and (3) determining how to best improve a facility or operation.	
Step 1b: Determine who needs to be involved in the decision	
Description: Identify and solicit involvement from key stakeholders who (1) should be involved in making the decision or (2) will be affected by actions resulting from the decision-making process.	
Step 1c: Identify the options available to the decision maker	
Description: Describe the choices available to the decision maker. This will help focus efforts only on issues likely to influence the choice among credible alternatives.	
Step 1d: Identify the factors that will influence the decision (including risk factors)	
Description: Few decisions are based on only one factor. Most require consideration of many factors, including costs, schedules, risks, etc., at the same time. The stakeholders must identify the relevant decision factors.	
Step 1e: Gather information about the factors that influence stakeholders	
Description: Perform specific analyses (e.g., risk assessments and cost studies) to measure against the decision factors.	

Step 2: Perform the Risk Assessment

Step 2a: Establish the risk-related questions that need answers

Description:

Decide what questions, if answered, would provide the risk insights needed by the decision maker.

Step 2b: Determine the risk-related information needed to answer the questions

Description:

Describe the information necessary to answer each question posed in the previous step. For each information item, specify the following:

- Information type needed
- Precision required
- Certainty required
- Analysis resources (staff-hours, costs, etc.) available

Step 2c: Select the risk analysis tool(s)

Description:

Select the risk analysis tool(s) that will most efficiently develop the required risk-related information.

Step 2d: Establish the scope for the analysis tool(s)

Description:

Set any appropriate physical or analytical boundaries for the analysis.

Step 2e: Generate risk-based information using the analysis tool(s)

Description:

Apply the selected risk analysis tool(s). This may require the use of more than one analysis tool and may involve some iterative analysis (i.e., starting with a general, low-detail analysis and progressing toward a more specific, high-detail analysis).

Step 3: Apply the Results to Risk Management Decision Making

Step 3a: Assess possible risk management options

Description:

Determine how the risks can be managed most effectively. This decision can include (1) accepting/rejecting the risk or (2) finding specific ways to reduce the risk.

Step 3b: Use risk-based information in decision making

Description:

Use the risk-related information within the overall decision framework to make an informed, rational decision. This final decision-making step often involves significant communication with a broad set of stakeholders.

Step 4: Monitor Effectiveness Through Impact Assessment

Description:

Track the effectiveness of actions taken to manage risks. The goal is to verify that the organization is getting the expected results from its risk management decisions. If not, a new decision-making process must be considered.

All Steps: Facilitate Risk Communication

Description:

Encourage two-way, open communication among all stakeholders so that they will:

- Provide guidance on key issues to consider
- Provide relevant information needed for assessments
- Provide buy-in for the final decisions

Appendix B
Hazard Identification Guidesheet

HAZARD	EXAMPLE SOURCES	INITIATING EVENT	POTENTIAL CONSEQUENCES
Acoustic Energy	Equipment noise Ultrasonic cleaners	Reciprocating motion equipment	Cracking and breaking of brittle materials
		Irregular motion of rotating parts	Loosening of bolts or other fastened parts
		Irregular or cyclic motion during transportation	Breakage of lead wires, filaments, and supporting parts
		Pneumatic or hydraulic shock (water hammer)	Personnel fatigue
		Vibrating tools	Inability to read instruments or to activate controls
		Misaligned equipment in motion	Color fading
		Lack of vibration isolators	Damage to hearing
		Loose or undersized mountings	Interference with communications
		Bottoming or failure of shock mounts	Decreased corrosion resistance
		Pump or blower cavitation	Metal fatigue and other changes in crystalline structure
		High-velocity fluid hitting a surface or object that can vibrate	Involuntary reaction to sudden loud noise
		Sonic booms and other shock waves	Static electricity generated between susceptible surfaces
		Explosion and violent ruptures	Chattering of spring-type contacts, valves, and pointers
		Scraping of hard surfaces against each other	Loss of calibration of monitoring devices and other instruments
		Lack or failure of sound isolation devices such as mufflers	Possible false readings on pointer-type devices
		Escaping high-velocity gas	Crazing and flaking of finishes

HAZARD	EXAMPLE SOURCES	INITIATING EVENT	POTENTIAL CONSEQUENCES
Toxic/Corrosive/Reactive Materials	Acetone Fluorides Carbon monoxide Lead Ammonia and compounds Asbestos Trichlorethylene Dusts and particulates Pesticides/herbicides/insecticides Bacteria Beryllium and compounds Chlorine and compounds Decontamination solutions Sandblasting Cyanides Metal plating Arsenic Mercury Acetylene Methane Chromates Acid Caustics "Natural" chemicals (soil, air, water) Acids Bases Organic solvents Heavy metals *Note: See SARA Title III "List of Extremely Hazardous Chemicals"*	Insufficient ventilation in occupied, enclosed space Atmospheric pollution by industrial, automobile, or other exhausts Ingestion of toxic or contaminated materials or food Outgassing of gases at low pressures in confined spaces Drum corrosion Breech of containment due to material failure, overpressurization, thermal stress, corrosion, chemical reaction, mechanical damage, etc.	Effects on nervous system (narcosis, anesthesia, paralysis, nerve damage) Annoyance or nausea caused by foul odors Reduction in personnel efficiency or capabilities Destruction of vegetation Irritation of eyes, nose, throat, or respiratory passages Loss of containment Damage to: • Respiratory system • Blood system • Body organs • Skin damage (dermatitis)

HAZARD	EXAMPLE SOURCES	INITIATING EVENT	POTENTIAL CONSEQUENCES

Flammable Materials	Cellulose (plastics)
	Packing materials
	Rags
	Gasoline (storage and in vehicles)
	Coolant oil
	Diesel fuel
	Grease
	Hydrogen (including battery banks)
	Gases (other)
	Solvents
	Wood
	Methane
	Ethane
	Kerosene
	Fuel oil
	Hydrazine, monomethyl
	Hydrazine
	Coal
	Cleaning agents
	Lubricants
	Welding gases
	Paints and varnishes
	Hydraulic fluids
		Combustible mixture with initiating source such as:
		
		• Open flame:
		  – Welding processes and flame cutting
		  – Matches, smoking
		  – Gas heaters
		  – Fired-process equipment and furnaces
		  – Nearby fires
		
		• Sparks
		  – Electrical equipment
		  – Static discharges
		  – Lightning
		  – Mechanical (hot solid particles)
		  – Chemical (carbon particles in exhausts)
			Heat and high temperature effects
			Loss of oxygen
			Production of toxic gases and smoke
			Production of corrosive materials
			Destruction of material and resources
			Burns to personnel
			Explosions
			Equipment rendered inoperative
			Carbonization and contamination of material

HAZARD	EXAMPLE SOURCES	INITIATING EVENT	POTENTIAL CONSEQUENCES

Flammable Materials (cont'd)	Elastomers (seals and gaskets)
	Furnishings and upholstery
	Plastics
	Refuse and trash
	Other organic materials
	Normally nonflammable metals in finely powdered form:
	• Aluminum
	• Magnesium
	• Titanium
	• Iron
	Afterburning of products of combustion of engine operations or incomplete combustion of organic materials
		Combustible mixture heated to autoignition temperature by:
		• External heat sources:
		  – Electrical heaters or hot plates
		  – High-wattage electronic equipment
		  – Boilers, radiators, steam lines, and equipment
		  – Exhaust stacks and manifolds
		  – Hot process equipment
		  – Friction (mechanical, aerodynamic)
		• Inadequate dissipation of chemical reaction heat (spontaneous ignition):
		  – Oily rags
		  – Sawdust, excelsior
		  – Subbituminous coal, lignite, peat
		  – Powdered plastics
		Adiabatic compression of flammable gas mixture
		Hypergolic mixtures
		Pyrophoric reactions with air
		Reactions with water-sensitive materials
		Enriched oxygen atmospheres	

HAZARD	EXAMPLE SOURCES	INITIATING EVENT	POTENTIAL CONSEQUENCES

Explosive/Pyrophoric Materials	Caps
	Primer cord
	Dynamite
	Powder metallurgy
	Dusts
	Hydrogen (including battery banks and water decomposition)
	Nitrates
	Electric squibs
	Peroxides-superoxides
	Solvents
	Ordnance or munitions systems
	Oxidizers
	Any fuel system
	High-pressure equipment
	Cryogenic liquid system
	Highly reactive materials
	Compression
	Monopropellants
	Acetylene
	Propane
	Methane
	Ozone
	Other gases (e.g., carbon monoxide)
	Nitro-compounds (e.g., nitro methane and nitro glycerine)
		Activation of:
		• Explosives
		• Propellants in containers or cases
		• Combustible gases in confined spaces
		• Fine dusts and powders
		• Combustible gases or liquids:
		  — In high concentrations
		  — In presence of strong oxidizers
		  — At high temperatures
		
		Activation of confined solid propellants that are:
		• Cracked, defective, contain voids, improperly bounded, at excessive temperature, have excess oxidizer or burning catalyst
		
		Afterburning of confined combustion products
		
		Delayed combustion in a firing chamber
		
		Hot soaking of solid propellants
		
		Overpressurization of boilers, accumulators, or other pressure vessels
		
		Failure of compression device such as an engine or compressor cylinder
			Rupture of pressurized container
			
			Blast, causing:
			• Overpressures (impulse energy)
			• Collapse of nearby containers
			• Damage to structures and equipment
			• Propagation of other explosions
			
			Fragmentation, causing:

HAZARD	EXAMPLE SOURCES	INITIATING EVENT	POTENTIAL CONSEQUENCES
Explosive/Pyrophoric Materials (cont'd)		Warning of closed cryogenic (or other) system containing highly volatile fluid	
		Fuel, lubricant, or solvent in contact with a strong oxidizer	
		Ignition of hydrogen from battery or fuel cell charging	
		Contact between water or moisture with water-sensitive materials such as molten sodium, potassium, or lithium; concentrated acids or alkalis; or similar substances, especially in containers or other restricted volume	

HAZARD	EXAMPLE SOURCES	INITIATING EVENT	POTENTIAL CONSEQUENCES
Electrical Energy	Battery banks Diesel units High voltage lines Transformers Wiring Switchgear Underground wiring Cable runs Service outlets and fittings Pumps Motors Heaters Power tools Small equipment Thermoelectric power Fuel cells Lightning Static electricity Solar cells	Accidental contact with live circuit through: • Erroneous connection • Faulty connector or connection • Touching bare conductor • Cutting through insulation • Inadequate insulation • Deteriorated insulation • Defective electrical tool or appliance Lightning strike Short circuit caused by: • Erroneous connection	Shock:
Electrical Energy (cont'd)		Breakdown of dielectric Stray currents from: • Lightning strikes • Static electricity discharge • Inductive or capacitive coupling • Misapplied test equipment power • Cross-connections • Electrostatic discharge • Electrolytic action Power source failure caused by: • Failure of basic energy converter • Power surges causing fuse opening or circuit breaker activation • System overloading • Short-circuiting	Discharges in air may cause: • Ignition of combustibles • Surface damage to metals and other materials • Buildup and welding of contacts

HAZARD	EXAMPLE SOURCES	INITIATING EVENT	POTENTIAL CONSEQUENCES
Thermal Energy • High temperature	Convection Heavy metal weld preheat Exposed steam pipes Electric heaters Fire boxes Leading melting pot Electric wiring and equipment Furnaces Plasma-arc torch Any fuel-consuming process Exothermic chemical process Solar energy Moving parts	Fire or explosion Other exothermic chemical reaction Heat engine operation Nuclear reaction Electrical resistance losses Inductive heating Friction between moving parts Internal friction due to repeated bending or repeated impacts Gas compression Exposure to sun or artificial light Inadequate heat dissipation capacity Hot spots due to coolant fluid being blocked Cooling system failure Welding, soldering, brazing, or metal cutting Proximity to operations involving large amounts of heat (radiation, convection, conduction) Immersion in hot fluid	Ignition of combustibles Initiation of other reactions Increased reactivity Melting of metals and thermoplastics Charring of organic materials Reduced strength of metals and other materials Distortion and warping of parts Weakening of soldered seams Increased evaporation rate of liquids (fuels, lubricants, toxic liquids) Expansion causing binding or loosening of parts Increased gas diffusion Reduced relative humidity Increased absolute humidity Breakdown of chemical compounds Burns to personnel Reduced personnel efficiency Heat cramps, strokes, and exhaustion Peeling of finishes, blistering of paint Decreased viscosity of lubricants Increased electrical resistance Changes in other electrical characteristics Softening of insulation and sealants Opening or closing of electrical contacts due to expansion

HAZARD	EXAMPLE SOURCES	INITIATING EVENT	POTENTIAL CONSEQUENCES
Thermal Energy (cont'd)		Lack of insulation from thermal sources Organic decay processes Capacitive heating Cooler bypassed	Premature operation of thermally activated time-delay devices
• Low temperature	Any heat-removal process Refrigerating or cryogenic systems Autorefrigeration of compressed or liquified gases	Cold climate or weather Endothermic reactions Exposure to heat sink Mechanical cooling processes Gas expansion Joule–Thomson effect Rapid evaporation Immersion in cold fluid Inadequate heat supply Heat loss by radiation, conduction, or convection	Reduced reaction rate Frostbite or cryogenic burns Freezing of liquids Icing of operating equipment Condensation of moisture and other vapors Reduced viscosity Gelling of lubricants Increased brittleness of metals Loss of flexibility of organic materials Contraction effects, especially opening of cracks in metal Delayed ignition in furnaces and combustion chambers Combustion instability in engines Changes in electrical characteristics Jamming or loosening of moving parts due to contraction Delayed operation of thermally activated time-delay devices

HAZARD	EXAMPLE SOURCES	INITIATING EVENT	POTENTIAL CONSEQUENCES
Kinetic Energy • Kinetic-Linear	Scraping equipment Cars Trucks Buses Forklifts Carts Dollies Conveyors Earth removal equipment Railroad Surfaces Obstructions Shears Presses Crane loads in motion Pressure relief valve blowdown Power-assisted operations	Acceleration: • Vehicle, body, or fluid being set into motion or increasing speed • Any falling body or dropped object • Vehicle on downgrade • Uncontrolled loss of altitude or height • Impact of another body • Force applied against an unrestrained body • Turbulence: clear air, thunderstorm, thermal, terrain • Sudden violent maneuver • Sudden valve opening in a pressure system Deceleration:	Injury to personnel A person may be: • Hit by an object set in motion by a sudden change in velocity • Thrown against a hard surface during sudden deceleration • Thrown backward during sudden forward acceleration • Thrown against ceiling in a sudden drop or maneuver Overloading and deformation of structural members
• Kinetic-Rotational	Centrifuges Motors Pumps/fans Cafeteria equipment Laundry equipment Gears Shop equipment (grinders, saws, brushes, etc.) Floor polishers Robot-assisted operations Turbines		

HAZARD	EXAMPLE SOURCES	INITIATING EVENT	POTENTIAL CONSEQUENCES
Potential Energy • Pressure – High pressure	Boilers Heated surge tanks Autoclaves Test loops and facilities Gas bottles containing compressed gases Pressure vessels Coiled springs Stressed members Gas receivers Hydraulic systems Pneumatic systems Cryogenic systems Pressurized containers Compressors	Overpressurization Connection to excessively high pressure system Excessively high combustion rate in combustion chamber with restricted exhaust passage No pressure relief valve or vent Faulty pressure relief valve or vent Heating gases in closed containers Heating fluids with high vapor pressures Warming cryogenic liquids in a closed or inadequately vented system Impact Blast Failure or improper release of connectors Inadequate restraining devices High acceleration of liquid system Water hammer (hydraulic shock)	Container ruptured or crushed Blast Fragments of ruptured container blown about Unsecured container propelled by escaping gas Eye or skin damage due to blowing dirt or other solid particles Whipping about of hoses Increase in chemical reaction rate Increase in burning rate Lung and ear damage Cutting by thin, high-pressure jets Shock Leaks in lines and equipment designed for lower pressures Blowout of seals and gaskets Permanent deformation of metals Excessively rapid motion of hydraulically or pneumatically activated equipment

HAZARD	EXAMPLE SOURCES	INITIATING EVENT	POTENTIAL CONSEQUENCES
– Low pressure	Vacuum Systems	Inadequate design against implosion forces Rapid condensation of gas in a closed system Decrease in gas volume by combustion Cooling of hot gas in a closed system Draining without adequate venting	Unbalanced forces Pressurized vessel collapses Pressurized vessel bursts Increased leakage if differential pressure increases
• Mass/gravity/height	Stairs Lifts Cranes Bucket and ladder Trucks Slings Hoists Elevators Jacks Scaffolds and ladders Crane cabs Pits Excavations Elevated doors Suspended loads		

Appendix C
Human Error:
A Marine Safety Example

By Dr. Anita M. Rothblum

U.S. Coast Guard Research & Development Center

Over the last 40 years or so, the shipping industry has focused on improving ship structure and the reliability of ship systems in order to reduce casualties and increase efficiency and productivity. We've seen improvements in hull design, stability systems, propulsion systems, and navigational equipment. Today's ship systems are technologically advanced and highly reliable.

Yet, the maritime casualty rate is still high. Why? Why is it, with all these improvements, we have not significantly reduced the risk of accidents? It is because ship structure and system reliability are a relatively small part of the safety equation. The maritime system is a *people* system, and human errors figure prominently in casualty situations. About 75-96% of marine casualties are caused, at least in part, by some form of human error. Studies have shown that human error contributes to:

- 84-88% of tanker accidents

- 79% of towing vessel groundings

- 89-96% of collisions·

- 75% of allisions[3]

- 75% of fires and explosions[3]

Therefore, if we want to make greater strides towards reducing marine casualties, we must begin to focus on the types of human errors that cause casualties.

One way to identify the types of human errors relevant to the maritime industry is to study marine accidents and determine how they happen. Chairman Jim Hall of the National Transportation Safety Board (NTSB) has said that accidents can be viewed as very successful events. What Chairman Hall means by "successful" is that it is actually pretty difficult to create an accident (thank goodness!). Accidents are not usually caused by a single failure or mistake, but by the confluence of a whole series, or chain, of errors. In looking at how accidents happen, it is usually possible to trace the development of an accident through a number of discrete events.

A Dutch study of 100 marine casualties found that the number of causes per accident ranged from 7 to 58, with a median of 23. Minor things go wrong or little mistakes are made which, in and of themselves, may seem innocuous. However, sometimes when these seemingly minor events converge, the result is a casualty. In the study, human error was found to contribute to 96 of the 100 accidents. In 93 of the accidents, multiple human errors were made, usually by two or more people, each of whom made about two errors apiece. But here is the most important point: *every human error* that was made was determined to be a *necessary condition* for the accident. That means that if just one of those human errors had *not* occurred, the chain of events would have been broken, and *the accident would not have happened*. Therefore, if we can find ways to prevent some of these human errors, or at least increase the probability that such errors will be noticed and corrected, we can achieve greater marine safety and fewer casualties.

Types of Human Error

What do we mean by "human error"? Human error is sometimes described as being one of the following: an incorrect decision, an improperly performed action, or an improper lack of action (inaction). Probably a better way to explain human error is to provide examples from two real marine casualties.

The first example is the collision of the M/V SANTA CRUZ II and the USCGC CUYAHOGA, which occurred on a clear, calm night on the Chesapeake Bay. Both vessels saw each other visually and on radar. So what could possibly go wrong? Well, the CUYAHOGA turned in front of the SANTA CRUZ II. In the collision that ensued, 11 Coast Guardsmen lost their lives. What could have caused such a tragedy? Equipment malfunctions? Severe currents? A buoy off-station? No, the sole cause was human error.

There were two primary errors that were made. The first was on the part of the CUYAHOGA's captain: he misinterpreted the configuration of the running lights on the SANTA CRUZ II, and thus misperceived its size and heading. When he ordered that fateful turn, he thought he was well clear of the other vessel. The second error was on the part of the crew: they realized what was happening, but failed to inform or question the captain. They figured the captain's perception of the situation was the same as their own, and that the captain must have had a good reason to order the turn. So they just stood there and let it happen. Another type of human error that may have contributed to the casualty was insufficient manning (notice that this is not an error on the part of the captain or crew; rather, it is an error on the part of a "management" decision-maker who determined the cutter's minimum crew size). The vessel was undermanned, and the crew was overworked. Fatigue and excessive workload may have contributed to the captain's perceptual error and the crew's unresponsiveness.

The second example is the grounding of the TORREY CANYON. Again we have clear, calm weather—this time it was a daylight transit of the English Channel. While proceeding through the Scilly Islands, the ship ran aground, spilling 100,000 tons of oil.

At least four different human errors contributed to this accident. The first was economic pressure, that is, the pressure to keep to schedule (pressure exerted on the master by management). The TORREY CANYON was loaded with cargo and headed for its deep-water terminal in Wales. The shipping agent had contacted the captain to warn him of decreasing tides at Milford Haven, the entrance to the terminal. The captain knew that if he didn't make the next high tide, he might have to wait as much as five days before the water depth would be sufficient for the ship to enter. This pressure to keep to schedule was exacerbated by a second factor: the captain's vanity about his ship's appearance. He needed to transfer cargo in order to even out the ship's draft. He could have performed the transfer while underway, but that would have increased the probability that he might spill a little oil on the decks and come into port with a "sloppy" ship. So instead, he opted to rush to get past the Scillies and into Milford Haven in order to make the transfer, thus increasing the pressure to make good time.

The third human error in this chain was another poor decision by the master. He decided, in order to save time, to go *through* the Scilly Islands, instead of *around* them as originally planned. He made this decision even though he did not have a copy of the *Channel Pilot* for that area, and even though he was not very familiar with the area.

The final human error was an equipment design error (made by the equipment manufacturer). The steering selector switch was in the wrong position: it had been left on autopilot. Unfortunately, the design of the steering selector unit did not give any indication of its setting at the helm. So when the captain ordered a turn into the western channel through the Scillies, the helmsman dutifully turned the wheel, but nothing happened. By the time they figured out the problem and got the steering selector back on "manual", it was too late to make the turn, and the TORREY CANYON ran aground.

As these two examples show, there are many different kinds of human error. It is important to recognize that "human error" encompasses much more than what is commonly called "operator error". In order to understand what causes human error, we need to consider how humans work within the maritime system.

The Maritime System: People, Technology, Environment, and Organizational Factors

As was stated earlier, the maritime system is a *people* system (Fig. 1). People interact with technology, the environment, and organizational factors. Sometimes the weak link is with the people themselves; but more often the weak link is the way that technological, environmental, or organizational factors influence the way people perform. Let's look at each of these factors.

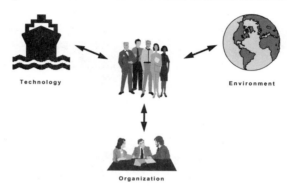

Fig. 1. The Maritime System Is A *People* System

First, the people. In the maritime system this could include the ship's crew, pilots, dock workers, Vessel Traffic Service operators, and others. The performance of these people will be dependent on many traits, both innate and learned (Fig. 2). As human beings, we all have certain abilities and limitations. For example, human beings are great at pattern discrimination and recognition. There isn't a machine in the world that can interpret a radar screen as well as a trained human being can. On the other hand, we are fairly limited in our memory capacity and in our ability to calculate numbers quickly and accurately—machines can do a much better job. In addition to these inborn characteristics, human performance is also influenced by the knowledge and skills we have acquired, as well as by internal regulators such as motivation and alertness.

- **Knowledge**
- **Skills**
- **Abilities**
- **Memory**
- **Motivation**
- **Alertness**

Fig. 2. The Maritime System: People

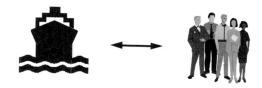

• Anthropometry
• Equipment layout
• Information display
• Maintenance

• **Reach, strength, agility**
• **Perception & comprehension**
• **Decision-making**
• **Safety & performance**

Fig. 3. The Maritime System: Effect of Technology on People

The design of technology can have a big impact on how people perform (Fig. 3). For example, people come in certain sizes and have limited strength. So when a piece of equipment meant to be used outside is designed with data entry keys that are too small and too close together to be operated by a gloved hand, or if a cutoff valve is positioned out of easy reach, these designs will have a detrimental effect on performance. Automation is often designed without much thought to the information that the user needs to access. Critical information is sometimes either not displayed at all or else displayed in a manner which is not easy to interpret. Such designs can lead to inadequate comprehension of the state of the system and to poor decision making.

The environment affects performance, too (Fig. 4). By "environment" we are including not only weather and other aspects of the physical work environment (such as lighting, noise, and temperature), but also the regulatory and economic climates. The physical work environment directly affects one's ability to perform. For example, the human body performs best in a fairly restricted temperature range. Performance will be degraded at temperatures outside that range, and fail altogether in extreme temperatures. High sea states and ship vibrations can affect locomotion and manual dexterity, as well as cause stress and fatigue. Tight economic conditions can increase the probability of risk-taking (e.g., making schedule at all costs).

Finally, organizational factors, both crew organization and company policies, affect human performance (Fig. 5). Crew size and training decisions directly affect crew workload and their capabilities to perform safely and effectively. A strict hierarchical command structure can inhibit effective teamwork, whereas free, interactive communications can enhance it. Work schedules which do not provide the individual with regular and sufficient sleep time produce fatigue. Company policies with respect to meeting schedules and working safely will directly influence the degree of risk-taking behavior and operational safety.

As you can see, while human errors are all too often blamed on "inattention" or "mistakes" on the part of the operator, more often than not they are symptomatic of deeper and more complicated problems in the total maritime system. Human errors are generally caused by technologies, environments, and organizations which are incompatible in some way with optimal human performance. These incompatible factors "set up" the human operator to make mistakes. So what is to be done to solve this problem? Traditionally, management has tried either to cajole or threaten its personnel into not making errors, as though proper motivation could somehow overcome inborn human limitations. In other words, the human has been expected to adapt to the system. *This does not work.* Instead, what needs to be done is to *adapt the system to the human.*

The discipline of human factors is devoted to understanding human capabilities and limitations, and to applying this information to design equipment, work environments, procedures, and policies that are compatible with human abilities. In this way we can design technology, environments, and organizations which will work *with* people to enhance their performance, instead of working *against* people and degrading their performance. This kind of *human-centered* approach (that is, adapting the system to the human) has many benefits, including increased efficiency and effectiveness, decreased errors and accidents, decreased training costs, decreased personnel injuries and lost time, and increased morale.

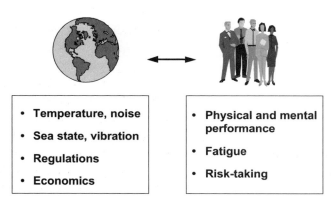

Fig. 4. The Maritime System: Effect of Environment on People

Fig. 5. The Maritime System: Effect of Organization on People

Human Factors Issues in the Marine Industry

What are some of the most important human factors challenges facing the maritime industry today? A study by the U.S. Coast Guard found many areas where the industry can improve safety and performance through the application of human factors principles. The three largest problems were fatigue, inadequate communication and coordination between pilot and bridge crew, and inadequate technical knowledge (especially of radar). Below are summaries of these and other human factors areas that need to be improved in order to prevent casualties.

Fatigue. The NTSB has identified fatigue to be an important cross-modal issue, being just as pertinent and in need of improvement in the maritime industry as it is in the aviation, rail, and automotive industries. Fatigue has been cited as the "number one" concern of mariners in two different studies. It was also the most frequently mentioned problem in a recent Coast Guard survey[9]. A new study has objectively substantiated these anecdotal fears: in a study of critical vessel casualties and personnel injuries, it was found that fatigue contributed to 16% of the vessel casualties and 33% of the injuries. More information on fatigue and how to prevent or reduce it can be found in subsequent chapters in this book.

Inadequate Communications. Another area for improvement is communications—between shipmates, between masters and pilots, ship-to-ship, and ship-to-VTS. An NTSB report stated that 70% of major marine collisions and allisions occurred while a State or federal pilot was directing one or both vessels. Better procedures and training can be designed to promote better communications and coordination on and between vessels. Bridge Resource Management (BRM) is a first step towards improvement.

Inadequate General Technical Knowledge. In one study, this problem was responsible for 35% of casualties[5]. The main contributor to this category was a lack of knowledge of the proper use of technology, such as radar. Mariners often do not understand how the automation works or under what set of operating conditions it was designed to work effectively. The unfortunate result is that mariners sometimes make errors in using the equipment or depend on a piece of equipment when they should be getting information from alternate sources.

Inadequate Knowledge of Own Ship Systems. A frequent contributing factor to marine casualties is inadequate knowledge of own ship operations and equipment. Several studies and casualty reports have warned of the difficulties encountered by crews and pilots who are constantly working on ships of different sizes, with different equipment, and carrying different cargoes. The lack of ship-specific knowledge was cited as a problem by 78% of the mariners surveyed[11]. A combination of better training, standardized equipment design, and an overhaul of the present method of assigning crew to ships can help solve this problem.

Poor Design of Automation. One challenge is to improve the design of shipboard automation. Poor design pervades almost all shipboard automation, leading to collisions from misinterpretation of radar displays, oil spills from poorly designed overfill devices, and allisions due to poor design of bow thrusters. Poor equipment design was cited as a causal factor in one-third of major marine casualties[5]. The "fix" is relatively simple: equipment designers need to consider how a given piece of equipment will support the mariner's task and how that piece of equipment will fit into the entire equipment "suite" used by the mariner. Human factors engineering methods and principles are in routine use in other industries to ensure human-centered equipment design and evaluation. The maritime industry needs to follow suit. This topic is discussed further in a subsequent chapter.

Decisions Based on Inadequate Information. Mariners are charged with making navigation decisions based on all available information. Too often, we have a tendency to rely on either a favored piece of equipment or our memory. Many casualties result from the failure to consult available information (such as that from a radar or an echo-sounder). In other cases, critical information may be lacking or incorrect, leading to navigation errors (for example, bridge supports often are not marked, or buoys may be off-station).

Faulty standards, policies, or practices. This is an oft-cited category and covers a variety of problems. Included in this category is the lack of available, precise, written, and comprehensible operational procedures aboard ship (if something goes wrong, and if a well-written manual is not immediately available, a correct and timely response is much less likely). Other problems in this category include management policies which encourage risk-taking (like pressure to meet schedules at all costs) and the lack of consistent traffic rules from port to port.

Poor maintenance. Published reports[3,11] and survey results[9] expressed concern regarding the poor maintenance of ships. Poor maintenance can result in a dangerous work environment, lack of working backup systems, and crew fatigue from the need to make emergency repairs. Poor maintenance is also a leading cause of fires and explosions[3].

Hazardous natural environment. The marine environment is not a forgiving one. Currents, winds, and fog make for treacherous working conditions. When we fail to incorporate these factors into the design of our ships and equipment, and when we fail to adjust our operations based on hazardous environmental conditions, we are at greater risk for casualties.

Summary

This chapter has introduced the concept of "human error". We have seen that human error (and usually multiple errors made by multiple people) contributes to the vast majority (75-96%) of marine casualties, making the prevention of human error of paramount importance if we wish to reduce the number and severity of maritime accidents. Many types of human errors were described, the majority of which were shown not to be the "fault" of the human operator. Rather, most of these errors tend to occur as a result of technologies, work environments, and organizational factors which do not sufficiently consider the abilities and limitations of the people who must interact with them, thus "setting up" the human operator for failure. Human errors *can* be reduced significantly. Other industries have shown that human error can be controlled through *human-centered design*. By keeping the human operator uppermost in our minds, we can design technologies, work environments, and organizations which support the human operator and foster improved performance and fewer accidents.

Endnotes

[1] Transportation Safety Board of Canada. (1994) Working Paper on Tankers Involved in Shipping Accidents 1975-1992.

[2] Cormier P.J. (1994) *Towing Vessel Safety: Analysis of Congressional and Coast Guard Investigative Response to Operator Involvement in Casualties Where a Presumption of Negligence Exists.* Masters Thesis, University of Rhode Island.

[3] Bryant D.T. (1991) *The Human Element in Shipping Casualties.* Report prepared for the Dept. of Transport, Marine Directorate, United Kingdom.

[4] U.K. P&I Club (1992). The United Kingdom Mutual Steam Ship Assurance Association (Bermuda) Limited. *Analysis of Major Claims.*

[5] Wagenaar W.A. and Groeneweg J. (1987) Accidents at sea: Multiple causes and impossible consequences. *Int. J. Man-Machine Studies, 27,* 587-598.

[6] This means that half the accidents had 7-23 causes and the other half of the accidents had 23-58 causes.

[7] Perrow C. (1984) *Normal Accidents: Living with High-Risk Technologies.* Basic Books, pp. 215-218.

[8] Perrow C. (1984) *Normal Accidents: Living with High-Risk Technologies.* Basic Books, pp. 182-184.

[9] U.S. Coast Guard (1995) *Prevention Through People: Quality Action Team Report.* Washington, DC: U.S. Coast Guard.

[10] Marine Transportation Research Board [MTRB]. (1976) *Human Error in Merchant Marine Safety.* Washington, DC: National Academy of Science. AD/A-028 371.

[11] National Research Council [NRC]. (1990) *Crew Size and Maritime Safety.* Washington, DC: National Academy Press.

[12] A "critical" vessel casualty was defined as a vessel casualty in which there was significant damage to the vessel or property, or in which the safety of the crew was at risk.

[13] McCallum M.C., Raby M., and Rothblum A.M. (1996) *Procedures for Investigating and Reporting Human Factors and Fatigue Contributions to Marine Casualties.* Washington, D.C.: U.S. Dept. of Transportation, U.S. Coast Guard Report No. CG-D-09-97. AD-A323392

[14] National Transportation Safety Board [NTSB]. (1981) *Major Marine Collisions and Effects of Preventive Recommendations.* Report No. NTSB-MSS-81-1.

Appendix D
Acronym List and Glossary of Terms

Acronym List

AOR	Area of responsibility
CCF	Common cause failure
COTP	Captain of the port
DOI	Document of Inspection
ETA	Event tree analysis
FMEA	Failure modes and effects analysis
FMECA	Failure modes, effects, and criticality analysis
FTA	Fault tree analysis
HAZMAT	Hazardous materials
HAZOP	Hazard and operability analysis
HRA	Human reliability analysis
IBA	Inflatable buoyancy apparatus
LNG	Liquefied natural gas
LOA	Line of assurance
MSO	Marine Safety Office
MTS	Marine Transportation System
OCMI	Officer in charge of marine inspections
ORM	Operational risk management
PAWSA	Ports and Waterways Safety Assessment
PIW	Person in the water
PQS	Personnel qualification standard
PrHA	Preliminary hazard analysis

PrRA	Preliminary risk analysis
R&D Center	Research and Development Center
R2TAR	Rank Risk, Target Risk
RCM	Reliability-centered maintenance
RIN	Risk index number
SAR	Search and rescue
SEH	Safety, environmental, and health
WET	Waterway evaluation tool
WISE	Worker and instruction safety evaluation

Glossary

Accident	Possible result of a deviation; a loss of interest
Accident sequence or scenario	One pathway from an initiating event (incident) to an unwanted result
Actions	Suggestions for design changes, procedural changes, or further study
AND gate	A Boolean logic element used to develop fault trees. The output event related to this gate exists only if all of the input events exist at the same time.
Asphyxiant hazard	The potential for one or more materials to prevent organisms from using oxygen
Basic events	The lowest level of resolution in a fault tree
Branch point	A graphical illustration used when constructing an event tree, usually of two possible outcomes when a line of assurance is challenged
Causal factors	Key events or conditions, such as human error or equipment failure, that may result in an accident. Causal factors are usually (1) an initiating event for an accident, (2) a failed safeguard, or (3) a reasonable safeguard that was not provided.
Cause	An event that, if not mitigated, may result in an accident
Certainty	The confidence that the risk information generated from a risk assessment is accurate
Change analysis	A risk assessment technique that logically identifies risk impacts and risk management strategies in situations where change is occurring
Checklist analysis	An analysis technique that evaluates a situation against existing guidelines in the form of one or more checklists
Chemical asphyxiants	Materials that prevent organisms from using oxygen
Chemical reactant hazard	The potential for one or more materials to chemically combine, or to self-react, and produce unwanted consequences
Combustible or flammable hazard	The potential for one or more materials to quickly react with an oxidant, releasing energy in the form of heat and light
Common cause failure	Failures that occur because of the same root causes, thus defeating many layers of protection at the same time
Consequences	Unwanted events that can negatively affect subjects of interest
Corrosivity hazard	The potential for one or more materials to chemically burn body tissues, especially the skin and eyes, or to excessively erode or dissolve materials of construction or emergency response equipment
Coupling factors	Factors that lead to common cause failures
Data uncertainty	Lack of confidence in the information used to provide risk assessment results
Decision maker	An individual or group, such as a management team, that uses risk assessment results to make risk-based decisions

Glossary (continued)

Deficiency	The failure of a system or operation to perform as it was intended
Demanded events	One or more events that act, or should act, to interrupt the chain of events stemming from an initiating event or incident
Design intent	A planned action or function that should be performed, based on the design specifications
Deviation	An unusual condition or situation that has the possibility to result in an accident
Effects	Measurable negative impacts on subjects of interest
Electrical energy hazard	The potential for unwanted consequences resulting from contact with, or failure of, manufactured or natural sources of electrical voltage or current. Electrical energy hazards include lightning, electrical charges, short circuits, stray currents, and loss of power sources
Error-likely situation	A situation or characteristic of a system or activity that makes human errors more likely
Error-likely situation checklist analysis	An analysis technique that uses a checklist of human factors issues, either general or specific, on areas of an activity to find current strengths and weaknesses
Event tree analysis (ETA)	An analysis technique that uses decision trees to graphically model the possible results from an initiating event that is able to produce an accident of interest
Event and causal factor charting	A written or graphical description for the time sequence of contributing events of an accident
Explosion hazard	The potential for one or more substances to release energy over a short period of time, creating a pressure wave that travels away from the source
Failed safeguards	Planned protections that fail to prevent or reduce unwanted effects
Failure modes and effects analysis (FMEA)	An approach best suited to reviews of mechanical and electrical hardware systems. The FMEA technique (1) considers how the failure modes of each part of the system can cause system performance problems and (2) makes sure that appropriate safeguards against such problems are in place.
Failure modes, effects, and criticality analysis (FMECA)	A quantitative version of FMEA
Fault tree analysis (FTA)	A deductive analysis that uses Boolean logic to graphically model how logical relationships among equipment failures, human errors, and external events can combine to cause specific accidents of interest
Frequency	The expected number of occurrences, per unit time, of an accident
Frequency range	A lower and upper limit of an accident's estimated frequency of occurrence
Hazard and operability (HAZOP) analysis	An approach that uses a logical process with special guide words to suggest ways in which system sections can deviate from design intents. This approach helps ensure that safeguards are in place to help prevent system performance problems.
	Situations, conditions, characteristics, or properties that create the potential for unwanted consequences

Glossary (continued)

Hazards	An analysis that evaluates the possibility for human actions or inactions that are outside the limits set by a system or operating envelope
Human error analysis	An analysis tool that is specialized and graphical, similar to event tree analyses. It is designed for evaluating series of operations that people perform. This technique considers human errors and recovery actions, as well as equipment failures.
Human reliability analysis event tree	
	The process of tracking the effectiveness of actions taken to better manage risks. The goal is to be sure that the organization is benefiting from the actions as intended.
Impact assessment	
	Visual, audible, physical, and odor clues, etc., that suggest to a crew member or some other inspector or troubleshooter that a failure mode has occurred
Indications	The event in an accident sequence that begins a chain of events that will result in one or more unwanted consequences unless planned demanded events are successful. Also called an incident.
Initiating event	
	Consequences that have a great impact on the organization
Issues of concern	Unwanted events or conditions identified during an analysis that must be addressed or corrected, but did not lead to the loss event of interest
Items of note	The potential for unwanted consequences resulting from motion of materials, equipment, or vehicles
Kinetic energy hazard	A protective system or human action that may respond to an initiating event or incident
Line of assurance	Any action, state, or condition in which a system is not meeting one or more of its design intents and causes unwanted consequences
Loss	Lack of confidence in the models used in both the overall decision-making structure and in risk assessments that support decision making because of the level of detail in the models and scope limits
Model uncertainty	
	A Boolean logic element used to build fault trees. The output event related to this gate exists if at least one of the input events exists.
OR gate	A screening assessment tool that uses historical information to identify and rank the most notable areas of interest for more evaluation
Pareto analysis	The potential for unwanted consequences resulting from (1) high pressures other than explosions (e.g., normal operational pressures), (2) low pressures (e.g., vacuum conditions), or (3) mass, gravity, or height (e.g., lifting operations)
Potential energy hazard	
	A broad study, used in the early stages of system design, that focuses on (1) identifying apparent hazards, (2) assessing the seriousness of accidents that could occur involving the hazards, and (3) identifying safeguards for lowering the risks of the hazards. The PrHA focuses on identifying weaknesses early in the life of the system, thus saving time and money that could be needed for major redesign if the hazards were found later.
Preliminary hazard analysis (PrHA)	
	A streamlined, accident-centered risk assessment approach. The main objective of the technique is to identify the risk of significant accident scenarios.

Glossary (continued)

Preliminary risk analysis (PrRA)	Expressible in terms of quality or kind (e.g., too much, too little, very high, very low)
Qualitative	Expressible in terms of quantity (e.g., 100 deaths)
Quantitative	Suggestions and action items for (1) reducing the risk of a deviation or (2) providing further evaluation of specific issues
Recommendations	A ranking technique that uses features of a system or activity to calculate index numbers that can be used to compare different systems and activities. The numbers can, in some cases, be related to absolute risk estimates.
Relative ranking/risk indexing	A measure combining an undesirable event's frequency and consequence
Risk	Activities that ensure the success of a risk assessment project. These activities include defining the scope of the risk assessment, identifying participants, preparing for the risk assessment, directing the meetings, documenting the meetings, writing the report, and implementing recommendations.
Risk assessment project management	The process of understanding (1) what bad things can happen, (2) how likely they are to happen, and (3) how severe the effects may be
Risk assessment	The interactive process of exchanging information and opinion among individuals, groups, and institutions about a risk or possible risk to human health or the environment
Risk communication	A quantitative measure of risk used in many risk assessment methods
Risk index number (RIN)	Actions that minimize risk within acceptable limits
Risk management	A matrix showing the risk profile of issues analyzed; each cell in the matrix provides the number of accident sequences having that frequency and consequence
Risk matrix	A process that organizes information about the possibility for one or more unwanted outcomes into a broad, orderly structure that helps decision makers make better management choices
Risk-based decision making	An analysis technique that defines the most basic causes of an event that can be reasonably identified and that management has control or influence to fix
Root cause analysis	Equipment, procedural, and administrative controls in place to help (1) prevent a situation from occurring or (2) reduce the effects if the situation does occur
Safeguards	Reasonable protections that were not provided but that could have prevented or reduced unwanted effects
Safeguards not provided	Determining at a general level that an item is of low risk and will not need to be assessed in detail
Screening	An evaluation that determines how (1) a change in one component of a system affects the entire system or (2) a change in one aspect of a risk assessment affects overall results
	Nontoxic gases that replace oxygen necessary to support life

Glossary (continued)

Sensitivity analysis
An individual or group that determines the need for a risk assessment. The sponsor is responsible for obtaining results from the risk assessment, and usually has a specific use for the results.

Simple asphyxiants

Sponsor
Individuals or groups possibly affected by the decision. Stakeholder input into the decision-making process is important for reaching the best decisions and improving acceptance for the process and its results.

Stakeholders
Individuals or groups who take part in the risk assessment, providing expert knowledge and experience about operations, layouts, and possible problems

Planned protections that successfully prevent or reduce unwanted effects

Subject matter experts
The potential for very hot or cold temperatures to produce unwanted consequences affecting people, materials, equipment, or work areas

Successful safeguards
The potential for one or more materials to cause biological damage to surrounding organisms by being absorbed through the skin, inhaled, eaten, or injected

Thermal hazard

Events that are not further developed in a fault tree

Toxic hazard
An option that offers more value to the user by providing some important benefit while sacrificing a previously existing, less important benefit

Undeveloped events
A brainstorming risk assessment approach that uses broad, loosely structured questioning to (1) suggest system upsets that may result in accidents and (2) make sure that safeguards against those accidents are in place

Value tradeoff

What-if analysis
A specialized form of HAZOP analysis for assessing human activities through the use of guide words customized for human factors issues, including issues historically addressed through job task analysis

Use of a team of experts to review and vote on competing options

Worker instructor and safety evaluation (WISE)

Voting method

Government Institutes Mini-Catalog

PC #	ENVIRONMENTAL TITLES	Pub Date	Price*
629	ABCs of Environmental Regulation	1998	$65
672	Book of Lists for Regulated Hazardous Substances, 9th Edition	1999	$95
4100	CFR Chemical Lists on CD ROM, 1999-2000 Edition	1999	$125
512	Clean Water Handbook, Second Edition	1996	$115
581	EH&S Auditing Made Easy	1997	$95
673	E H & S CFR Training Requirements, Fourth Edition	2000	$99
825	Environmental, Health and Safety Audits, 8th Edition	2001	$115
548	Environmental Engineering and Science	1997	$95
643	Environmental Guide to the Internet, Fourth Edition	1998	$75
820	Environmental Law Handbook, Sixteenth Edition	2001	$99
688	EH&S Dictionary: Official Regulatory Terms, Seventh Edition	2000	$95
821	Environmental Statutes, 2001 Edition	2001	$115
4099	Environmental Statutes on CD ROM for Windows-Single User, 1999 Ed.	1999	$169
707	Federal Facility Environmental Compliance and Enforcement Guide	2000	$115
708	Federal Facility Environmental Management Systems	2000	$99
689	Fundamentals of Site Remediation	2000	$85
515	Industrial Environmental Management: A Practical Approach	1996	$95
510	ISO 14000: Understanding Environmental Standards	1996	$85
551	ISO 14001: An Executive Report	1996	$75
588	International Environmental Auditing	1998	$179
518	Lead Regulation Handbook	1996	$95
608	NEPA Effectiveness: Mastering the Process	1998	$95
582	Recycling & Waste Mgmt Guide to the Internet	1997	$65
615	Risk Management Planning Handbook	1998	$105
603	Superfund Manual, 6th Edition	1997	$129
685	State Environmental Agencies on the Internet	1999	$75
566	TSCA Handbook, Third Edition	1997	$115
534	Wetland Mitigation: Mitigation Banking and Other Strategies	1997	$95

PC #	SAFETY and HEALTH TITLES	Pub Date	Price*
697	Applied Statistics in Occupational Safety and Health	2000	$105
547	Construction Safety Handbook	1996	$95
553	Cumulative Trauma Disorders	1997	$75
663	Forklift Safety, Second Edition	1999	$85
709	Fundamentals of Occupational Safety & Health, Second Edition	2001	$69
612	HAZWOPER Incident Command	1998	$75
662	Machine Guarding Handbook	1999	$75
535	Making Sense of OSHA Compliance	1997	$75
718	OSHA's New Ergonomic Standard	2001	$95
558	PPE Made Easy	1998	$95
683	Product Safety Handbook	2001	$95
598	Project Mgmt for E H & S Professionals	1997	$85
658	Root Cause Analysis	1999	$105
552	Safety & Health in Agriculture, Forestry and Fisheries	1997	$155
669	Safety & Health on the Internet, Third Edition	1999	$75
668	Safety Made Easy, Second Edition	1999	$75
590	Your Company Safety and Health Manual	1997	$95

Government Institutes

4 Research Place, Suite 200 • Rockville, MD 20850-3226
Tel. (301) 921-2323 • FAX (301) 921-0264
Email: giinfo@govinst.com • Internet: http://www.govinst.com

Please call our customer service department at (301) 921-2323 for a free publications catalog.

CFRs now available online. Call (301) 921-2355 for info.

*All prices are subject to change. Please call for current prices and availablity.

Government Institutes Order Form

4 Research Place, Suite 200 • Rockville, MD 20850-3226
Tel (301) 921-2323 • Fax (301) 921-0264
Internet: http://www.govinst.com • E-mail: giinfo@govinst.com

4 EASY WAYS TO ORDER

1. Tel: **(301) 921-2323**
Have your credit card ready when you call.

2. Fax: **(301) 921-0264**
Fax this completed order form with your company purchase order or credit card information.

3. Mail: **Government Institutes Division**
ABS Group Inc.
P.O. Box 846304
Dallas, TX 75284-6304   USA

Mail this completed order form with a check, company purchase order, or credit card information.

4. Online: **Visit http://www.govinst.com**

PAYMENT OPTIONS

❏ **Check** *(payable in US dollars to ABS Group Inc. Government Institutes Division)*

❏ **Purchase Order** *(This order form must be attached to your company P.O. Note: All International orders must be prepaid.)*

❏ **Credit Card** ☐ *VISA* ☐ *MasterCard* ☐ *AMERICAN EXPRESS*

Exp. ____ / ____

Credit Card No. _____

Signature _____

(Government Institutes' Federal I.D.# is 13-2695912)

CUSTOMER INFORMATION

Ship To: (Please attach your purchase order)

Name _____

GI Account # *(7 digits on mailing label)* _____

Company/Institution _____

Address _____
(Please supply street address for UPS shipping)
_____

City _____ State/Province _____

Zip/Postal Code _____ Country _____

Tel ( ) _____

Fax ( ) _____

E-mail Address _____

Bill To: (if different from ship-to address)

Name _____

Title/Position _____

Company/Institution _____

Address _____
(Please supply street address for UPS shipping)
_____

City _____ State/Province _____

Zip/Postal Code _____ Country _____

Tel ( ) _____

Fax ( ) _____

E-mail Address _____

Qty.	Product Code	Title	Price

30 DAY MONEY-BACK GUARANTEE
If you're not completely satisfied with any product, return it undamaged within 30 days for a full and immediate refund on the price of the product.

Subtotal _____
MD Residents add 5% Sales Tax _____
Shipping and Handling (see box below) _____
Total Payment Enclosed _____

SOURCE CODE: BP03

Shipping and Handling	Sales Tax
Within U.S:	Maryland 5%
1-4 products: $6/product	Texas 8.25%
5 or more: $4/product	Virginia 4.5%
Outside U.S:	
Add $15 for each item (Global)	